How to Run Your Own Court Case

A practical Guide to Representing Yourself in Australian Courts and Tribunals: Non-Criminal Cases

Nadine Behan

16pt

Copyright Page from the Original Book

A Redfern Legal Centre Publishing book
<www.rlcp.org.au>

Published by
University of New South Wales Press Ltd
University of New South Wales
Sydney NSW 2052
AUSTRALIA
<www.unswpress.com.au>

© Nadine Behan 2009
First published 2009

This book is copyright. Apart from any fair dealing for the purpose of private study, research, criticism or review, as permitted under the Copyright Act, no part of this book may be reproduced by any process without written permission. Inquiries should be addressed to the publisher.

National Library of Australia
Cataloguing-in-Publication entry
    Author: Behan, Nadine.
    Title: How to run your own court case: a practical guide to representing yourself in Australian courts and tribunals/Nadine Behan.
    ISBN: 978 1 921410 83 3 (pbk.)
    Notes: Includes index.
    Subjects: Civil procedure – Australia.
        Pro se representation Australia – Popular works.
        Self help (Law) – Australia.
        Civil procedure – Popular works.
        Pro se representation – Popular works.
        Self help (Law) – Popular works.
    Dewey Number: 347.94

Design Josephine Pajor-Markus
Cover iStock
Printer Ligare

This book is printed on paper using fibre supplied from plantation or sustainably managed forests.

Note for the reader
While every effort has been made to make the information contained in this book as up to date and accurate as possible to reflect the laws and the legal system of Australia as at August 2008, its contents are not intended as legal advice. Use it as a guide only and be sure to obtain legal advice for your specific legal problem.

TABLE OF CONTENTS

HOW TO RUN YOUR OWN COURT CASE	i
Foreword	ii
Acknowledgments	iv
Introduction	v
How to use this book	viii
1: Why represent yourself?	1
2: A word about lawyers	4
3: Should you get a lawyer?	19
4: Do you have a case at all?	32
5: Should your case end up in court?	34
6: Where to go for help	40
7: Our legal system	48
8: The litigation process	72
9: The golden rules of litigation	77
10: Preparing your case part 1	80
11: Preparing your case part 2	127
12: Preparing your case part 3	169
13: The hearing	233
14: The result	243
Glossary of terms	257
Useful resources	273
Back Cover Material	324
Index	325

HOW TO RUN YOUR OWN COURT CASE

Nadine Behan BA LLB Grad Dip (Communication) worked for ten years as a barrister and solicitor at a community legal centre, specialising in non-criminal law. Her work involved conducting litigation, advising clients and supervising a legal advice clinic, which assisted people who were running their own cases. In the course of her work, she realised the great need for a book like this. Nadine has one son and now writes and lives in Sydney.

Foreword

Nadine Behan has written a book that will be invaluable to the many people who find themselves parties to litigation and have no lawyer. Some tribunals exclude lawyers, many deal with subject matters too small to justify the expense of lawyers, and unhappily many litigants in important matters such as child contact simply cannot afford to have a lawyer but are denied legal aid. To all of these people, this book is a friend in need.

Even when one can afford a lawyer, it is nice to know what is happening. This book will tell you. Every step in litigation is carefully but simply explained, and illustrated by useful examples. In addition there is a glossary of legal terms, which will help the amateur understand what is happening.

The book covers all of Australia and concludes with very useful lists of Dispute Resolution Services, Legal Aid Centres and Community Legal Centres where the reader, if necessary, may obtain further assistance.

Nadine is one of those lawyers who specialised in helping the needy at community legal centres and through this book she continues to help the many persons who cannot afford to pay legal fees.

However, I might add that even veteran advocates might pick up a point or two from reading this book.

Chester Porter QC

Acknowledgments

I would like to thank Jane Franklin Hall, University of Tasmania, for the Visiting Fellowship granted for the writing of this book. Thanks also to Jack Bowers, Fran Moore, Alex Bailiff, Alex Hackett, Stephen Langman, Hugh Jorgensen, Chester Porter QC, Stephanie Thomas, Adriana D'Addario, Maz Round, Iain Brady, Suzie Phillips, Jeanne Ryckmans, Judith Johnston, Carol Enderby, Bruce Rosen, Jude Wood, Marie-Louise Taylor, Heather Cam, Elspeth Menzies, Katherine Lane, Sir Anthony Mason, Leo Loomans, my sisters Kim and Paula and, most importantly, my son Dylan and my mum Vera Behan.

Introduction

Are you suing someone? Being sued? Are you facing family court proceedings? Appealing a government decision? Trying to recover a debt? Perhaps you want to resolve a dispute with a neighbour, a colleague or ex-employer. Or you might be finally putting your rights to the test by starting a consumer or environmental action. These are all examples of non-criminal legal action, or civil litigation.

If you're not a lawyer and you want to run your own noncriminal case in a court or tribunal, then this book is written for you. It applies Australia-wide to all types of civil litigation and it applies whether you are the one bringing the action or the one defending an action brought against you. Whether it's a tenancy dispute in Western Australia, a family law case in Canberra, a debt claim in Tasmania or the appeal of a local council decision in New South Wales, this book will show you how to run the best possible case on your own.

How to Run Your Own Court Case will guide you step-by-step through the litigation process. It will tell you what you want to know about making a claim, defending a claim, collecting your evidence, researching the law and preparing your presentation for the hearing.

Its methods are practical and effective. It explains how to approach a case systematically and examine it from a legal perspective. It breaks down complex procedures into simple and achievable building blocks, with outlines, case studies, important tips and golden rules. Along the way, it familiarises you with our legal system, identifies how and where to get help and equips you with the skills, knowledge and understanding needed to represent yourself with confidence and know-how.

This book does not aim to be a law textbook or to give you a law degree. What it does is show you how you can run an excellent case on your own and how not being a lawyer can be used to its greatest advantage.

If you decide to use a lawyer or already have one, this book will help you understand what is going on with your case. It can assist you in dealing with your lawyer and with the legal proceedings generally and it will improve the quality of the decisions you need to make during the case.

How to Run Your Own Court Case will prove useful too if you are a law student or a new lawyer facing your first civil cases by helping you get your bearings while you gain experience in litigation. As with all good instruction manuals, it won't give you all the answers but it does give you the ways to find them.

How to use this book

There are as many ways to run a case as there are cases. This book shows you just one; adapt it to suit your needs. However, it does not apply to criminal matters.

How to Run Your Own Court Case aims to build your skills and knowledge steadily, so it's best if you first read it from beginning to end. The basic information contained in the first half of the book provides the grounding for the later, more technical parts. Important terms appear in bold type the first time they are used, and are defined in the glossary of terms.

Just as every case is different and every type of court and tribunal is different, so the level of preparation that's needed will vary. The level provided in this book represents the mid-range of preparation. If your case is a modest one, some of the requirements outlined might not be necessary. Likewise, if your case is complex, there may be extra requirements than those stated. As you proceed, you will become the best judge of the level of preparation that's appropriate for your case.

Not all cases are within our power or capabilities to manage on our own. This book will help you determine whether you need assistance. If you decide to use a lawyer, this book will help you choose one and then shows you how to make the most of them. Use it to inform yourself of what you can expect from your lawyer and from the legal system.

Lastly, this book endorses our legal system and the litigation process. You won't find any tricks or strategies here that undermine this process in order to win.

1

Why represent yourself?

There are many reasons why people represent themselves. For some it's a conscious decision. Others have little choice but to go it alone.

Your case might be a minor one and not worth the bother or the cost of a lawyer. Or you may have never used a lawyer and don't know where to find a good one. You might have had a bad experience with lawyers in the past and want more control this time. Or perhaps a lawyer or the right lawyer is out of your price range.

The most common reason for not using a lawyer is probably the cost. Private lawyers aren't cheap. And increasingly, legal representation from legal aid and other free services is becoming harder to get.

At the same time our lives are now so regulated that we're constantly being exposed to the law. Like never before, we need to be able to access the legal system directly, quickly and easily to deal with the increasing number of problems that are coming our way.

Thankfully, we don't need to be a lawyer or have a lawyer to use the legal system. In fact, our system is built on the idea that we are all equal before the law. With or without a lawyer, we can take our grievance to a court of law and we can expect it to be heard and judged fairly according to the law.

This is one of our most basic and powerful democratic rights and each time we test this right, without a lawyer, we test the legal system to deliver the same high quality of justice. Be assured, the legal system understands the importance of self-representation.

If your case is suited to self-representation or if you have no choice but to represent yourself, running your own case can offer many advantages. By giving you direct control, it can bring great personal satisfaction, increase your peace of mind and it may even improve the quality of the result that you're seeking.

When you represent yourself you're kept personally informed of developments and have access to the information you need to continually assess your case's merits and your options. This gives you greater power over conducting your case, and yourself, appropriately.

At the hearing you interact directly with the decision-maker and can ensure that the correct facts and the correct arguments are presented. You can fix errors, update details and query inconsistencies that only an interested party might notice.

These simple things are surprisingly important. They better equip the decision-maker to make a clear and accurate decision. In turn, this gives your case the greatest chance of success.

It stands to reason that in an appropriate case, with the right preparation and care, you can be your own best advocate. After all, you know your case better than anyone.

2
A word about lawyers

Lawyers are divided into two groups: **solicitors** and **barristers.**

Solicitors do a variety of general legal work including wills, conveyancing, advice-giving and litigation. They are the first stop if you have a legal problem.

Barristers are the specialists in litigation. They are members of what is called 'the Bar' and are the ones who wear a wig and gown (much like the judges). They stand up in court and do the talking. Most often they are the brains behind the legal arguments.

Working as a litigation team, the solicitor deals directly with the client, collects the evidence and prepares the paperwork; the barrister does the legal research, prepares the arguments and presents the case in court.

Much like doctors, where if you need a specialist you must see a GP first, so it is with lawyers. If you need a barrister you must see a solicitor first. The solicitor will assess whether to do the case alone or whether to enlist the services of a barrister.

Also like doctors, where a GP can perform minor or routine procedures and the surgeon does the major surgery, solicitors can do less important court appearances but the barristers do the complex court work.

In most Australian states there is an independent Bar consisting of barristers who do not do the work of solicitors. In others, like Tasmania and the ACT, generally speaking, a lawyer acts as both a solicitor and barrister.

Whether barrister or solicitor, we expect a lot from lawyers. We expect them to know everything there is to know about the law, the courts, documents, procedures and the jargon. We expect them to understand all the possibilities of a case and all its risks. We expect them to negotiate, argue, even bully, to advance our best interests. We expect them to know with precision when it's best to settle a case and when to press on with it.

On top of this, we expect them to juggle clients, paperwork, tough deadlines and demanding schedules and still give each case the same attention and care. We demand without hesitation that they keep abreast of all developments, be available to answer queries, keep us fully informed and that, at all times, they act faithfully on our instructions.

The theory's good, but reality is often quite different.

Realistically, a lawyer will have many of these capabilities but not all of them. Some lawyers are gifted thinkers but lousy organisers. Some have better people skills than legal skills. Some excel in court. Others are better negotiators.

But let's face it, with all their faults, lawyers can do things that even in our wildest dreams we cannot. Their special value lies in their ability to take a human problem, convert it into legal terms, problem-solve it in a highly skilled way and then professionally and dispassionately take the necessary action. This knack for thinking 'legally' and acting 'lawyerly' means, for complex legal problems, they can be indispensable.

If you decide to use a lawyer, getting the right lawyer isn't always as easy as it sounds. The Law Society in your state or territory can provide you with a current list of legal practitioners. The Yellow Pages of the telephone book will also give you plenty of choice. But the most common method is by word of mouth. When shopping around, try to get a lawyer who has experience with your type of case.

If you're on a low income, the Legal Aid Commission in each state and territory provides lawyers for some non-criminal matters, including family law. Eligibility depends on factors such as your income, the prospects of success of your case and the amount of resources the case will take up. You may also be expected to make a financial contribution to the case. You will find a list of Legal Aid contacts at the back of the book.

Many community legal centres offer free legal representation in limited cases. The case study below describes one instance. For more information about community legal centres and their range of services see chapter 6.

Like all professions, there are good and bad lawyers. So, if you decide to use one here are some tips to help you choose the right one:
- know your needs. For example, is your case a straightforward matter or do you need an expert? Is it urgent? What stage has it reached? How much money can you afford to spend on this case?

CASE STUDY MARIA'S APPEALS

Maria disagreed with a Centrelink decision and applied for a review. When the internal review was unsuccessful, Maria applied to the Social Security Appeals Tribunal.

Maria contacted a community legal centre called the Welfare Rights Centre for some assistance with the appeal. Although Welfare Rights wouldn't provide a lawyer for the case, they did advise her extensively about how to run the case on her own.

Maria contacted the Centre some months later. She had gone ahead

> with the appeal and had been successful. Now Centrelink was appealing that decision to the Administrative Appeals Tribunal and Maria didn't feel comfortable about running this more complex appeal on her own.
>
> The Welfare Rights Centre examined the case and the issues involved and decided to represent Maria at the Administrative Appeals Tribunal. They considered her case was a strong one and, if successful, would benefit others in Maria's situation.

- shop around. Ring and inquire about specialisation, fee per hour and your special requisites. Ask how often the lawyer runs your type of case;
- use interest groups or support groups that deal with your type of legal problem to steer you in the right direction for the most suitable lawyers;
- if a lawyer is recommended to you, ask about the lawyer's specialisation. A brilliant personal

injury lawyer, for instance, might be inexperienced at family law;
- have realistic and reasonable expectations of the level of service you want from your lawyer;
- be prepared to pay appropriately for effective legal work;
- understand that a lawyer's first duty is not to you – it is to the court. Do not ask anything of a lawyer that would compromise this;
- at the first appointment insist that the lawyer give a written estimate of fees and costs. In some states the law requires a **written costs agreement.** This sets out the billing arrangements between you and the lawyer. It usually covers matters like the lawyer's rate per hour and the ability to charge for **disbursements.** Disbursements are the expenses the lawyer needs to recoup, for example, filing fees, the cost of serving documents, fees for expert reports and any barrister's fees;
- at the first appointment, it's a good sign if the lawyer does most or all of the following:

- takes down the facts of the case;
- reads the paperwork thoroughly;
- outlines your options;
- gives time frames;
- discusses any risks;
- explains the next steps;
- explains what will be required of you in the case;
- discusses your prospects of success.

To gain the greatest benefit from your lawyer, it's important to instruct them properly. For the first appointment, take all relevant paperwork with you and work out beforehand any important questions you need to ask. You can use the list above. Also, know what you want or need to resolve the case in a way that satisfies you.

Ask them how they propose to run the case, what law and arguments they'd be relying on. Ask them about the hearing. Ask about the prospects of settling the case without a hearing. Ask about time frames for documents. Ask what will be needed of you or from you and by what date. Discuss their fee and the written costs agreement.

CASE STUDY JACK TRAINS HIS LAWYER

Jack had known his lawyer for a long time and trusted him with his family law matter. He started becoming concerned when months went by without hearing any word of the progress of the case. He tried ringing the lawyer's office several times and leaving messages. After several attempts to contact him without a response, the messages became more urgent. Still no return call from the lawyer.

Then Jack wrote a short note asking for an update on his case explaining that he was worried. When this didn't work, Jack gave his lawyer one last chance. Although Jack valued the lawyer, he needed a lawyer who would not cause him such worry.

Without further delay, Jack put his detailed concerns in writing to the lawyer. He stated the number of times he'd called, the messages he'd left, and the amount of time he'd waited for a reply. He also stated that, although reluctantly, he was now considering changing lawyers and that if he did not hear from him within seven days he would pay what was owing for the work done, get his documents back and take his business elsewhere.

Luckily, the lawyer contacted Jack within time and apologised for his silence and delay, giving him a complete update on the case and explaining that no further action was expected until the return date for the subpoenas. The lawyer promised to contact Jack as soon as he had something to report.

Two weeks later the lawyer rang giving details of the information gained from the documents obtained from the subpoenas. From this, they discussed the next steps for the hearing and made some decisions about strategies. Jack was able to give proper instructions and they agreed to speak again two weeks before the hearing.

> With things back on track in his lawyer-client relationship, Jack was able to return his attention to other concerns in his life and approach the upcoming hearing with restored confidence.

A successful lawyer-client relationship is about teamwork. Just as you need a good lawyer, the lawyer too needs a good client.

Throughout the case, deal with your lawyer professionally. Provide them with requested information promptly. When they need a decision from you, instruct them clearly. Contact them only when necessary, but keep in touch with what stage your case is up to and what's happening.

Understand that time is money. You may think it's nice that your lawyer is having such a long, friendly chat with you on the telephone, but understand that you are probably the one paying for it. Better to save their time and your money by having clear and specific questions for them when you call.

If you have constant difficulty contacting your lawyer or if you become dissatisfied with their level of service, before you decide to change lawyers, try putting your concerns in writing to them.

There are several disadvantages to changing your lawyer during a case. Often lawyers do not like taking on someone else's work. They may not have run the case the same way if they had had it from the start. They may not agree with the direction it has taken. There can be complications in relation to changing the solicitor's details for service of documents. And you will need to pay your lawyer for their services so far, before they will agree to release your documents to you or another lawyer.

Nevertheless, if your written concerns to your lawyer are not addressed satisfactorily, you may wish to take your business elsewhere or complete the case yourself. If you believe your concerns warrant it, you may also make a complaint about the lawyer to the Law Society in your state or territory.

If you cannot afford a lawyer but need their help for your case, consider using them for specific aspects of the case. For example you might try engaging a lawyer to:
- give a written opinion on the issues involved in the case, the merits of the case or whether you should proceed with it;
- draft the initial **application** or **defence;**
- present your case at the hearing only. (You would need to attend to all other aspects of preparation of the case yourself.)

Not all lawyers would agree to working on just one aspect of a case. You may need to shop around.

No word about lawyers is complete without mentioning the other party's lawyer. When you represent yourself and the other party has engaged a lawyer, you will need to deal directly with the lawyer, rather than the party.

Most lawyers will treat you ethically and professionally, but it is not unknown for some to be less than co-operative towards self-represented litigants. Their tactics can include exaggerating the urgency of matters that favour them, over-use of legal jargon and unnecessary delays.

Like family, you can't choose the other party's lawyer and for better or worse, for the duration of the case, you're stuck with them. So remain calm, detached and business-like. Do not be distracted from your purpose by any problems you may have with the lawyer.

In the best interests of your case, always:
- behave well, act professionally and courteously;
- confirm any arrangements in writing;
- if you ask something of them, give them a reasonable time frame to comply;
- if they offer you something, ask for it in writing;
- try to contain any problems rather than escalate them. Get legal advice to help you deal with any obstacles that arise.

If you encounter serious problems with the lawyer, you may wish to make a formal complaint to the Law Society in your state or territory. Take this step only if you consider it necessary and have substantial grounds for the complaint.

3

Should you get a lawyer?

To determine whether you need a lawyer, consider the following factors:

How complex is your case?

At the outset any legal dispute can seem complex, especially to the parties involved. That it has even reached the litigation stage shows that the problem's been difficult to solve. But this doesn't mean necessarily that the case is legally complex.

Although the legal system has no shortage of complicated cases, the vast majority of cases are treated by the system as fairly simple, routine matters. This is because, to the trained eye, most cases can be reduced to one or two key issues.

The key issue might be: did you do what the law required? Or it might be: did the other party do what the law required? Or, does a certain law apply? Or has it been applied properly? Or do the facts justify a particular remedy?

For example, in a tenancy case the issue might be: is the landlord's notice to vacate valid? That is, did the landlord fulfil all the legal requirements in issuing the notice to vacate? In a family law matter, it might be whether the proposed arrangements for the children are in their best interests? In a debt matter, the issue might be about the exact amount of money owed, whether it is owed at all, or who actually owes it. For an appeal of a government decision about eligibility for a disability pension, the issue might be the degree of incapacity or whether the incapacity is permanent.

Begin assessing the complexity of your case by breaking it down in this way into its key element or elements. If your case involves more than one or two key elements, or if it involves a particularly slippery one, the case may not be a routine matter and it might be difficult to manage on your own.

Next, to help you judge its complexity, determine whether the key issues are issues of fact or issues of law. Don't assume that because it's a legal dispute it must involve a legal issue. Most cases are actually disputes about the facts, not about the law.

Issues of fact are things like: did you stop at the stop sign? Is the dog theirs? Did you agree to deliver the goods on Thursday? Did you deliver them on Thursday? Is your incapacity likely to last more than two years? Did the other party comply with the Family Court orders?

Issues of law, on the other hand, are about the mechanics of the actual law involved. Things like whether law X or law Y applies to your case, how it applies or what the particular wording in a law means, are all issues of law.

Disputes about the facts are often dealt with quite simply by the legal system. The decision-maker will decide the facts by weighing up the evidence that's presented. If the facts can be firmly established with good evidence, a smooth application of the law very often follows (but not always). These types of cases can be well suited to self-representation.

Disputes about the law, however, can become quite technical. Some legal issues can be treated in a straightforward manner using well-established case law. But if your case involves a particularly tricky interpretation or application of law, it may need the services of a well-trained and experienced legal mind. Consider getting a lawyer.

If your case involves several issues of fact or a combination of both issues of fact and law, it could need specialised help. The disputed events might stretch over long periods of time requiring substantial evidence or might attract several laws or changes to the law over time that call for technical interpretation, weighty argument or complex decision-making.

Some of these cases can break new ground and permanently change the legal landscape, but they can also be painstaking and slow, taking years to work their way through the court system as a series of appeals. For these types of cases you need a lawyer, a good one.

In assessing your case, do not confuse its legal complexity with its emotional complexity. A case that seems insurmountable emotionally might be quite straightforward legally.

Also, don't be tempted to judge its complexity by the number or sophistication of the lawyers your opponent uses. Having an impressive legal team might show how much money your opponent is willing to risk on the case or spend to intimidate you, but it gives no indication of the quality of that team, the quality of their case or the quality of the justice that will be delivered.

CASE STUDY McLIBEL CASE

The world-famous McLibel case defied all the rules. When the fast food chain McDonald's sued two environmental activists in Britain for libel over a pamphlet they were distributing that was critical of McDonald's, the activists had two choices: either apologise to McDonald's for the pamphlet or defend themselves in court. Without a university or legal education of any kind and without legal aid (legal aid was not available in Britain for a libel case), the two chose to defend the libel action and to represent themselves.

The case involved extensive scientific and other evidence about the food value of McDonald's meals, their labour practices and misleading claims about recycling as well as complex legal argument. Beginning with few resources, the pair obtained free legal advice and did much of their own legal research. In total they called 180 witnesses to prove their assertions. The case, lasting seven years, became the longest running case in British history and, although McDonald's technically won, the result was anything but a success for them.

Internationally and publicly embarrassed by the court action and by much of the information that was proved true, McDonald's declared that it would not try to collect the $40 000 that the court awarded. At any rate, the corporation's own legal costs for

> running the case were much greater, estimated at $10,000,000.
>
> This case is one example of what can be achieved by non-lawyers. However, the pair did not achieve it on their own. As the case grew, it captured public attention internationally and so its resources grew and it was sustained by the support of many volunteers, donations and a huge global campaign. It is unlikely the pair could have defended the case on such a scale without this support.

Which legal body will be hearing the case?

Often the particular court or tribunal hearing your case can be an indicator of whether you will need a lawyer.

The legal system has a hierarchy of legal bodies, with the lower or **inferior courts** generally hearing the minor matters. Courts like the Magistrates Court, Local Court and Small Claims Court are all inferior courts. These are accustomed to people representing themselves.

Many but not all tribunals are actually designed for people to represent themselves. If your case is being heard by a tribunal, check whether it is one of this type. These tribunals prefer to deal directly with the parties without escalating the formality, complexity, cost and delay that are often associated with the use of lawyers. Some tribunals even prohibit lawyers.

Also, some of the lower courts and tribunals are **no-costs jurisdictions.** This means that you can't recover your legal costs from your opponent if you win. This discourages the use of lawyers and reduces the likelihood that your opponent will use one. Check whether the court or tribunal you are using is a no-costs jurisdiction.

If your case is to be heard by a court in the upper levels of the hierarchy like the Supreme Court or High Court, seriously consider getting a lawyer. These **superior courts** are designed for lawyers, and specialised ones at that. Although it's not essential, be warned that extensive research as well as considerable time and effort can be required. These courts have elaborate procedures and strict formalities and their rules and paperwork can be gruelling.

Other legal bodies that are in-between in the court hierarchy – like the Family Court, Planning and Environment Court, Review or Appeals Tribunals – deal with both simple and complex matters. They are not, in themselves, an indicator of whether your case might be too difficult to run on your own.

How much money is involved?

The money factor affects your decision about a lawyer in a number of ways. Ask yourself:
- how much money is at stake in this case?
- can I afford a lawyer?
- will the lawyer cost more than the case is worth?

Although size is always relative, if your case involves a very large sum of money to you, give the decision about getting a lawyer some careful thought. You may wish to investigate a no-win-no-fee lawyer.

If the case is not worth too much financially, you may find it more satisfying to run the case yourself. Of course, if you use a lawyer and you win, you may be able to recover your legal costs from your opponent. But if you can't recover these costs, your sense of victory can quickly vanish once you get your lawyer's bill and do the sums and realise who's really winning from your case.

The amount of money at stake in the case may affect which court will hear the case, as some courts have limited powers. For example, Small Claims Courts and some tribunals can only hear disputes worth up to a certain amount. The next courts up in the hierarchy, for instance the Magistrates Court, may hear disputes for larger amounts, but they may also be limited.

Generally, the larger the amount involved the higher the court that hears the case. And the higher the court, the more complex are its procedures and so the more complex your case can become. The more complex the case, the greater the need for a lawyer.

What else is at stake?

It might not be just money that's at stake. Think carefully whether anything else is at risk. Perhaps it's quality of life, your home or family stability, better business opportunities or your future rights and entitlements. Weigh up these factors when deciding whether to get a lawyer. If you then decide to run the case yourself, you will do a better job being fully aware of the case's consequences.

If your case is one that's best described as 'it's not the money, it's the principle involved', unfortunately the 'principle' and the 'law' don't always mean the same thing. The principle may be important but the law is not always there to support it, so the chance of success in these cases is not necessarily high. Sheer perseverance and the eloquence of the affected party, though, can sometimes make the difference. Provided the case is a valid one, it can be well suited to self-representation.

Knowing your needs

At all stages of your case, be prepared to reassess whether you should get a lawyer or some type of extra legal help. If any of the following are happening, you may be getting out of your depth:
- if you can't deal with the paperwork involved;
- if you are not managing the deadlines for lodging documents;
- if, despite using every means you are capable of (including court remedies), you still find yourself powerless against the other party's delays;
- if, when you seek free legal advice, the legal questions involved leave the lawyer scratching their head;
- if, after you have lodged your claim, the other party makes a **strike-out application** or **motion** to the court concerning the claim, on the grounds that it has no reasonable basis or it is frivolous or vexatious. This may indicate you have real problems with the merits of your case.

Sometimes, though rarely, someone other than a lawyer may be able to represent you. Some tribunals, for example, allow other types of advocates like your social worker, disability advocate or aged or veterans' advocate to help you at the hearing. Check with the court or tribunal involved.

4

Do you have a case at all?

There isn't a legal remedy for every grievance. And if there is a remedy for your grievance, it may not be to your liking.

Before you get carried way with enlisting the legal system to fight the good fight for you, think about the actual substance of your case. The legal system deals with the law. It is not enough to argue injustice and unfairness in a court of law if there is no legal basis to your claims. You must have solid legal grounds on which to base your case.

Also you may have a number of serious grievances against your opponent, but they may not all be relevant to the case at hand. Spare yourself the time and angst. Define and isolate your grievances specifically so that you have the best chance of pursuing the grievance that you can succeed on and pursuing the right remedy for it.

This book and your research will help you determine whether your case has valid grounds. If at any stage you are still unsure, get legal advice. Chapter 6 'Where to go for help' lists where and how to get this advice.

Throughout the book you will be constantly reminded to reassess your case's merits. If at any time you become aware that you have no case at all to argue and you get legal advice that confirms this position, do not be afraid to back away. Check any liability you have incurred so far and the consequences of terminating the case. If you initiated the claim, you can withdraw it by notifying the other party and the court or tribunal and lodging the appropriate paperwork. If you are defending a claim against you, you can either accept full liability or try to negotiate a more suitable settlement.

5

Should your case end up in court?

This is the most important question of all. The legal system is not always the best option for resolving a dispute. Many disputes that end up in court could have been better solved by other means.

Community justice centres and dispute resolution services, for example, can perform miracles in helping people sort through entrenched conflict without resorting to the legal system. Whether the problem is at home or work, or with neighbours, tenants or business associates, these services help the parties negotiate their own agreement to end the conflict. And they find that these agreements work better than orders imposed by a court. A list of these services and their telephone numbers is included at the end of the book.

As an alternative to legal proceedings, or in addition to them, there are often other avenues to pursue as well. If your dispute is with a government agency or an institution that belongs to a certain industry like banking, credit, insurance, superannuation, telecommunications or energy, there are a range of state, federal and industry ombudsmen, as well as particular dispute resolution schemes that investigate and help resolve complaints, usually before they reach the litigation stage. Some of them cannot help you once legal proceedings have started. A list of these free services and their telephone numbers can be found at the end of the book. If your complaint concerns a government agency, you can also contact your local Member of Parliament (MP).

If you cannot resolve your dispute by other means and your case does need to go to court, there are certain advantages and disadvantages to using the legal process. The advantages are that it gives a powerful and impartial decision-maker the responsibility of finding a solution to the problem that you have not been able to solve. This provides an opportunity for you to air your grievance publicly and for the conflict to be contained and ended in a systematic and lawful way. If successful, the decision in your favour has the full force and authority of the law.

There are a number of disadvantages to using the legal system. First, in big letters with flashing lights:

WARNING! WARNING! WARNING! There is the risk that costs will be awarded against you if you lose the case.

This means that when the court issues its decision it may also order you to pay the other party's legal costs. Although they are usually calculated according to a fixed scale, these expenses can be considerable and can be more than what was at stake in the case. Take this risk very seriously when you are deciding whether or not to use the legal system.

Remember that some courts and many of the tribunals are no-costs jurisdiction where no such order about costs can be made and each party must bear their own legal expenses. Check this with the court or tribunal involved, as it is important to know their position regarding costs.

If you use the legal system and there is the risk of costs, try at an early stage to get written agreement from the other party that you will each pay your own costs in the case.

Another disadvantage of going to court is that sometimes the court process itself increases the conflict rather than ending it. Some parties use the legal system for retaliation rather than resolution and the emotional tit-for-tat can actually escalate. This creates a great deal of drawn-out and unnecessary hostility that could have been avoided if the matter had been solved by simpler means.

So if you are the one bringing the case to court, it's worthwhile to examine your motives. Are you seeking resolution, or revenge? Likewise, if you are the one deciding whether to defend a case brought against you, examine your motives. Are you pointlessly fighting a legally legitimate case?

Another disadvantage is that once you go to court, you may be stuck with the decision of that court. And you may not like it.

So try exhausting other possibilities before involving the legal system. If someone is threatening to sue you, try to negotiate with them before they take legal action. It may save you time and expense in the long run.

Likewise, before you sue for a debt, first issue a letter of demand. If this strategy works, it saves you considerable time, effort and uncertainty. If it doesn't then you can use the letter of demand in court to show that you've made reasonable efforts to obtain the money.

CASE STUDY HELEN'S LETTER

Helen was tired of making telephone calls asking for the money she was owed. She figured she might have to resort to the Small Claims Court to get results. But first she sent a letter of demand. In it she outlined the details of the debt with all the relevant dates and amounts and requested payment, giving 28 days to pay. She also stated in the letter that if payment wasn't received by that date, she wouldn't hesitate to take legal action to recover the money. She signed and dated the letter and kept a copy for her records.

The time limit did expire without Helen receiving her money, but Helen was satisfied now that she'd tried all the options. She felt much better about issuing a claim. Without delay, she obtained a claim form, filled it out and lodged it along with all the relevant documentation.

At court, Helen was able to easily establish her case. She provided all the paperwork concerning the debt and had maintained accurate records. The court was satisfied with her evidence and her attempts to recover the money and made an order in her favour for the amount owed as well as the filing fees.

6

Where to go for help

There are many free services available to help you prepare your case. Make the most of them. Use them to get started, to check details and answer queries as you go along and especially for advice whenever you need it. Keep a list of the most useful ones, for easy reference.

When seeking help, be sure to understand the difference between information and advice. Some agencies can provide legal information but not legal advice. For example, finding out generally about your legal rights is information, but applying the information to your particular situation to determine whether you have a valid case or not is advice. Answering queries about court forms and procedures is information, but telling you what to put on the form may amount to advice. Explaining what can be claimed in an application is information, determining what you should claim in your circumstances is advice.

For information and advice about your legal problem

There are excellent free or small fee legal services operated by community legal centres, Legal Aid and the Law Society in your particular state or territory. Some of these services offer legal representation, or ongoing help with the preparation of your case. Others give one-off legal advice, either instant telephone advice or face-to-face advice by appointment as well as general information and referral to other appropriate agencies. Although some of the services are means tested or attract a small fee, there is still a large range of free services available to all.

Start with the telephone book and when you access a service, ask where else you might get help. Ring around for the assistance you need.

Legal Aid offices in each state and territory offer various services, from telephone hotlines giving advice, face-to-face appointments, civil law clinics, help with preparing your own case as well as limited representation. A comprehensive list of their offices is included at the end of this book.

There are also 200 community legal centres operating across Australia. These centres come in all shapes and sizes. Some, like Redfern Legal Centre and Kingsford Legal Centre, give help on all types of legal matters to people in their locality. Others, like the Youth Law Centre and Women's Legal Centres, help specific sections of the community. Others again, like the Environment Law Centre, Arts Law Centre, Tenants Advice Services, Consumer Credit Legal Centres and Welfare Rights Centres, specialise in particular types of legal problems. A list of the various community legal centres is included at the end of this book.

For intensive assistance, try to find a community legal centre that deals with your specific problem. Or if your case is of significant public interest, you may be referred to another specialty centre, like a Public Interest Law Clearing House or the Public Interest Advocacy Centre that co-ordinates private lawyers who offer their services free for important test cases or where a public issue is at stake.

Some trade unions, insurance companies and even student organisations offer free advice and legal help to their members. Even your local MP can be an untapped legal resource.

There are also privately operated user-pays telephone advice services. Approach these with caution as the help they give can be quite general yet quite expensive.

Courts and tribunals give legal information but do not give legal advice. The exceptions are **chamber magistrates** and **registrars** who do give free legal advice.

For information about the court process

The websites of the federal, state and territory governments contain the best information about courts and tribunals. Begin at <www.australia.gov.au> or <www.gov.au>. These will take you to other government sites: <www.nsw.gov.au>, <www.nt.gov.au>, <www

.wa.gov.au>, and so on. Go to the Attorney-General or legal or justice section of the site.

Some of these sites provide links to helpful free services like the NSW Guide to Law on the Internet <www.lawaccess.nsw.gov.au> or <www.lawlink.nsw.gov.au>, with links to NSW law and justice agencies and services. Australian Law Online <www.law.gov.au> is another important site with links to all states and territories as well as contact details for helpful information services like the Regional Law Hotline and Family Law Hotline. As with all sites, they are constantly changing and new ones are being added.

For information about the court process you can usually also contact the staff at the registry of the court or tribunal that you'll be using. They process the paperwork, schedule the hearings and keep track of the progress of matters. This means they can help with your questions about forms, fees, time frames, time limits, the various stages of the process, the steps you need to follow and what the hearing will be like. They are your contact point also for specific queries about the progress of your case. They do not give legal advice.

The registry of the court or tribunal is also an important source of brochures, fact sheets, sample forms and information kits. Get them and read them.

To find legislation and cases

The Australasian Legal Information Institute website <www.austlii.edu.au> is the best free database for finding the law. It contains all Australian cases and legislation available on the internet, and has a good search engine.

Books and the internet

For helpful guides or law textbooks in a particular area of law try bookshops, your local library, the main city libraries, university libraries and law libraries at the law schools of major universities. Members of the public are able to use university libraries for study purposes, although they cannot borrow books. New South Wales, Victoria and Tasmania have legal library services specifically for the public. Their details are included at the end of this book.

Apart from complex legal textbooks, there are small summary books available on different areas of law. These are written for law students and are often quite easy to understand. Law dictionaries, too, can give useful explanations of legal terms. There are also guides to the law especially written for non-lawyers. *The Law Handbook* (UNSW Press), available for each state and territory, is the most extensive. As with any information obtained from books, always check that it is still up to date.

The internet can also be a valuable source of information on a particular area of law. With general searches on the internet of a certain topic, be careful that the information is relevant to and applies to your specific case. Later sections of this book will help you know how to tell, especially the next chapter ('Our legal system') and the later section on 'Legal research' in chapter 11 'Preparing your case part 2'.

With legal research of any kind, it's a good idea to get back-up legal advice to make sure you're on the right track.

7

Our legal system

What follows is a roller-coaster ride through our legal system. You don't need to study this too closely. Its aim is to give you, not a crash course in law, but a sketch of how law is made and the way the courts work. Use it to see where your case fits into the legal system.

Types of law

There are various types of law, for example, criminal, civil, family, commercial, international. The type of law affects the kind of remedy available, the methods used by the court, and the way the parties are treated. Here are some of the main ones.

If you are charged with an offence, the state is prosecuting you. This is **criminal law.** You are called the defendant; the other side is the prosecution. The case must be proved beyond reasonable doubt. Conviction can result in a fine, a criminal record and/or the loss of your freedom.

If you are suing or being sued, this is **civil law.** A 'lawsuit' is a civil action. Car accident compensation, for instance, other insurance claims, disputes with neighbours or tradesmen, tenancy matters, debts, consumer actions are all civil actions. The claim is usually for a sum of money and/or an order forcing or restraining particular action.

There is no single court or tribunal that deals with all civil actions. Depending on a number of factors, your case might be heard by a specialty tribunal like a Tenancy Tribunal that deals exclusively with a particular type of civil case or else a generalist court like the Local, Magistrates or Supreme Court that deals with both criminal and civil law. The factors that determine which legal body will hear your case include which state you live in, which law is involved, which remedy you're seeking and how much money the claim is for.

With civil law, the party bringing the action is usually called the **plaintiff** or **applicant** and the party opposing it is the **respondent** or **defendant.** To succeed you must prove your case on the balance of probabilities; that is, that it is more probable than not. This is easier than proving it beyond reasonable doubt.

Family law deals with the breakdown of family relationships. It offers a range of remedies to regulate the rights and obligations of spouses, the division of their property and the care of the children. Where children are involved, their interests are considered to be paramount.

In family law proceedings the party making the application to the court is called the applicant. The other party is the respondent. Generally, the test of proof for a family law case is the balance of probabilities and not proof beyond reasonable doubt.

Administrative law deals with the bureaucracy. An administrative law action is most often an appeal brought by a party against a government decision. For example, decisions about building approvals, veterans' entitlements, immigration, government pensions and benefits, obtaining government information and receiving government housing are all administrative decisions you can appeal against. Most but not all government decisions can be appealed.

The party appealing the government decision is called the applicant and the particular government department involved is the respondent. The appeal is usually heard by a tribunal. They look at the department's decision and decide if it is the correct one. The test of proof used is the balance of probabilities.

This book is suited to non-criminal matters such as civil, family and administrative law actions.

How law is made

Our legal system comes from Britain and has developed over many centuries. It combines law made both by parliament and the courts. Parliament enacts legislation and the courts apply it and enforce it. In applying it, the court decisions interpret what the law means.

As well, over the centuries, the courts have developed abundant case law in some areas to regulate certain behaviours and redress specific injustices without the aid of legislation. This case law is called the **common law.** These cases have grown into fairly self-contained bodies of law in their own right. For example, much of our law on issues like negligence, contracts, principles of natural justice and procedural fairness is found in the common law not legislation.

Courts and tribunals use their decisions as **precedents** to guide them in the future, in similar cases. These precedents are **binding** on that court or tribunal if the case is similar enough. This means the court or tribunal is bound to follow it. The case may even be binding on other courts and tribunals.

All legal bodies are connected in various ways in a hierarchy of appeal paths that stretches up to the most powerful federal court, the High Court. Decisions of one legal body can be binding on another that is lower in the hierarchy. For example, a Supreme Court's decision can be binding on a lower court like a Magistrates Court but will not be binding on the High Court.

How the system works

Power is divided between the local, state, territory and federal governments. They each have power over particular areas of law and have their own legal bodies to apply and enforce the laws they make.

The federal government, for instance, makes law on national matters like income tax, migration, social security, family law, veterans' affairs and defence, and has its own courts and tribunals, for example the Federal Court, Family Court, High Court. The state governments make law in areas like crime, roads and traffic, health and education, and have their own courts like the Magistrates Court, Court of Petty Sessions, Supreme Court. Then local governments make law about things like littering and parks and beaches.

There are some exceptions, with some powers being shared and some legal bodies shared. For example, the federal government makes law about health and education spending or, for another example, a state court may deal with your local council littering offence.

Some legal bodies deal with just one area of law, for example, the Family Court. Others deal with several different areas and are divided up internally. For instance, a state Supreme Court usually has a criminal, civil, commercial and appeal section. Likewise, the federal Administrative Appeals Tribunal has a general division and various others, like veterans, tax and social security.

The legal body hearing your case may use one or more decision-makers, but in non-criminal cases it rarely uses juries. In the lower courts, usually just one decision-maker, a magistrate, hears your case. Tribunals use one or more tribunal members. In the higher courts like the state Supreme Court, one or more judges are used. If your case is being heard in a higher court, by the 'full bench', this means three or perhaps five of its judges will be attending and deciding.

Types of legal approach

There are different approaches to the way a legal system can conduct its legal proceedings. The British, for example, use an **adversarial** approach whereas European countries use an **inquisitorial** approach. In Australia we inherited the adversarial approach from Britain, but over time aspects of the inquisitorial approach have been blended into parts of our legal system.

With an adversarial approach, the hearing is treated much like a debate or verbal jousting match between adversaries. The parties or their lawyers present the evidence and arguments and the decision-maker listens carefully and then decides the winner.

With this model, the responsibility for the evidence and arguments is on the parties. If a party neglects to raise their best evidence or present a crucial argument then it's bad luck for them and good luck for their opponent. The task of the decision-maker in this system is to ensure the hearing is conducted properly and to decide the case impartially according to the law.

Throughout the hearing, the decision-maker is often busy applying rules of procedure that govern the parties' (or their lawyer's) presentation. It is crucial for the decision-maker that the parties/lawyers adhere to the rules. A good example of this approach can be seen in the British television series 'Rumpole of the Bailey'.

> ## EXAMPLE OF A FORMAL ADVERSARIAL APPROACH
>
> It's almost 10am at the busy District Court complex. Courtroom 1 is hearing the civil matters. Two half-day hearings are listed for today and the lawyers and parties for the first one are already in court waiting to begin.
>
> The lawyers are seated at the Bar table in the middle of the courtroom facing the 'bench', where the judge will sit. The parties sit behind the lawyers in the front rows allotted for the general public. Behind the parties are a few other people who have drifted in to watch the proceedings.

At 10am precisely the court official goes towards the front of the court to a side door and loudly knocks twice on the door then opens it and the judge enters.

'All stand, please, and remain standing,' says the court official, and the lawyers, parties and public alike all get to their feet. 'This court is now in session. Please be seated,' he says and everyone quietly sits.

One of the lawyers at the Bar table stands. 'Parker, for the plaintiff,' he says, introducing himself and then sits back down. Another lawyer rises. 'Evans, for the respondent,' she says and sits.

'Yes,' acknowledges the judge. 'Now there are some procedural matters that must be dealt with before the trial can begin. I have a statement of claim with various annexures here filed on 16 March last year.'

Parker, the lawyer responsible for the statement of claim, stands. 'Yes, Your Honour.'

'Does that raise all the issues in your case, Mr Parker?'

'Yes, Your Honour.' Parker sits.

'There is a defence, filed on 14 May last year. Does that raise all the issues in defending that claim, Ms Evans?'

Ms Evans rises. 'Yes, Your Honour.'

'Is there to be any oral evidence adduced by your party, Mr Parker?'

Evans sits, Parker stands. 'Yes, Your Honour. There is my client and also his brother. And there are the following affidavits together with the affidavits in reply.' Mr Parker lists the various affidavits by name and date then sits.

Evans stands. 'My client has various objections to the contents of these affidavits, can we deal with those objections now?'

'In a moment, Ms Evans. Do you have any oral evidence, Ms Evans?'

'Yes, my client will give oral evidence, Your Honour.'

'Very well, we can deal with your objections now.'

'In relation to the first affidavit stated by my learned friend, I refer Your Honour to paragraph 24. My client objects to this paragraph on the ground that it is hearsay.'

'What do you have to say, Mr Parker? What principle of evidence are you relying on to allow this paragraph?'

Evans sits, Parker stands. 'It is a statement, Your Honour, by my client expressing his opinion of what happened.'

'Well, objection upheld. Paragraph 24 is to be struck out.'

Parker sits, Evans stands and proceeds with more objections. 'I refer Your Honour to Paragraph 32 and make the same objection.'

'Your response to the objection, Mr Parker?'

Evans sits, Parker stands. For the next few minutes the judge, Parker and Evans deal with the various objections so that the hearing can begin.

With this done, Parker stands again. 'The court is already familiar

> with this matter. Perhaps we can go straight to the evidence.'
> 'Yes,' agrees the judge.
> 'I call the witness, Percy William Todd,' says Parker and the court official rises and exits the courtroom through the main door to call the first witness...

An inquisitorial approach, on the other hand, treats a hearing as an inquiry into the case by the decision-maker. The parties or their lawyers still present their case, but the decision-maker plays a much more active role in directing the case not just the procedures and is not restricted by the lawyers' or parties' presentation. The decision-maker is free to question the witnesses directly, query the evidence and arguments, interrupt the lawyer's presentation and do whatever is necessary to clear away any obstacles to making the correct decision. With this approach, a good result can depend less on the parties' (or their lawyers') presentation and more on the inquiries of the decision-maker. With a purely inquisitorial approach, the decision-maker can entirely 'run the show'. The US television series 'Judge Judy' is one example of the inquisitorial method.

> ## EXAMPLE OF AN INFORMAL INQUISITORIAL APPROACH
>
> The applicant, Ms Black, is appealing a Centrelink decision that she is a member of a couple, as defined by the *Social Security Act 1991*. The Social Security Appeals Tribunal is hearing her appeal. It's 9.30am and the hearing begins with the Presiding Member introducing herself and the other tribunal members hearing today's case, to Ms Black. The hearing room is a small meeting room with a rather large table. Ms Black and the three tribunal members are all seated around the table.
>
> 'Ms Black,' says the Presiding Member, 'our job today is to take a fresh look at your Centrelink decision and to decide if it is correct. We have read the documents from Centrelink

setting out the decision and their reasons for it and today we will talk to you. Then after the hearing we will make a decision and send the written decision to you. That usually happens within 28 days.'

The Presiding Member continues. 'We would like you to feel entirely comfortable and to speak freely with us about your case. We have read the statutory declarations from your family and friends that you have given us as well as the various receipts for bills. We will get to those in a moment. You have also brought your sister here for us to speak with her. She will stay in the waiting room until we are ready to hear from her. The hearing today will take approximately an hour. If you are ready we can begin.'

'Yes,' replies Ms Black.

'Now, we have a few questions for you, to help us understand the exact nature of your relationship with Mr Brown...'

Both types of approach have advantages. Understanding the differences will help you know what to expect during your litigation.

As a general rule of thumb, the older higher courts in our legal system operate using the more formal adversarial system. Courtroom procedure can be elaborate and is followed closely and the decision-maker usually remains detached as the parties present their case.

The lower courts are also adversarial, but procedure is usually less elaborate and more flexible and with their need for faster, cheaper and simpler justice, most lower courts have developed a certain inquisitorial flavour. The decision-maker is often much more active in moving the hearing along and making inquiries directly of the parties and their witnesses.

Tribunals are a fairly new breed of legal institution in Australia and some of them, like the Social Security Appeals Tribunal, are based entirely on the inquisitorial model. Others are a blend of the inquisitorial and adversarial approach, with some being more adversarial, some more inquisitorial. The federal Administrative Appeals Tribunal, for example can be more adversarial, the NSW Administrative Decisions Tribunal is more inquisitorial. Although their powers may be considerable, tribunals generally put significant effort into trying to keep hearings informal, explaining things simply and putting the parties at ease as much as possible.

If you have a choice between using a court or a tribunal to hear your case, tribunals are generally less costly and more user friendly for self-represented litigants. So it may be better to choose the tribunal.

Legal remedies

The information contained in this section is meant as background and is probably much more than you will need. However, it will give you some idea of different remedies and the rules governing them.

Generally speaking, criminal law is about penalties and civil law is about remedies. The aim of civil law is not to penalise or punish the wrongdoer but to redress a wrong in a way that restores the parties to the position they would be in if the wrong hadn't occurred. To do this, civil law has developed a range of different remedies and rules about granting them.

Knowing which remedy (or remedies) is appropriate for which wrong depends on a number of factors. The particular type of legal problem, the particular relationship between the parties, the particular legal body that will be hearing the claim and, of course, the particular wrong that has occurred all affect the choice of remedy.

Legal remedies come from a variety of sources within civil law. They come from legislation, case law and the terms of the particular agreements that parties make. Often more than one source can apply at the same time.

Legislation can spell out what remedies can be granted. For example, under the NSW *Consumer Claims Act 1998,* when determining a consumer claim, the Consumer, Trader and Tenancy Tribunal can make orders to:
- pay compensation;
- fix defects in goods or services;

- supply particular goods or services;
- return or replace goods;
- refund all or part of the purchase price;
- declare that an amount of money is not owed;
- dismiss all or part of the claim.

The *Administrative Appeals Tribunal Act 1975* is another example of law that sets out the remedies available. This tribunal reviews decisions of the federal government and section 43 of the Act sets out the Tribunal's options. It can:
- affirm the decision;
- vary it;
- set it aside and make a substitute decision;
- remit the matter back to the department, the original decision-maker, for the decision to be made again (but often with guidance about how the decision needs to be made properly this time).

Agreements between parties, like leases and other types of contracts, also often contain the remedies that a court or tribunal will enforce if that contract is breached. A tenancy agreement, for example, will set out the particular course of action open to a party for a particular breach of that agreement.

Over the centuries, case law has also developed remedies for particular wrongs as well as principles that govern the application of remedies to each case. The types of damages available and the rules for assessing damages in civil law are two important examples of judge-made law. Another example is a number of remedies found in the body of law called **equity**.

Both the law of damages and the law of equity can be quite useful but also quite complex. If you are interested in investigating either of these further, you will need legal advice. What follows is a brief description of them.

As there are various types of damages and various rules regarding their measure and availability, not all types are available in all situations. Some types are as follows:
- in personal injury cases, **general damages** are for noneconomic loss like pain and suffering and loss of amenity of life, and **specific**

damages are for expenses like medical bills;
- **nominal damages** apply where the wrong has been proved but no actual monetary loss has resulted. These damages can amount to as little as $1;
- **compensatory damages** compensate for the actual loss suffered;
- **aggravated damages** can apply where the injury has been aggravated by the wrongdoer's behaviour, for example their cruelty;
- **exemplary damages** are awarded not just to compensate but to punish the wrongdoer.

In Australia, most damages awarded are compensatory. Aggravated and exemplary damages are uncommon.

There are rules, too, about the assessment of damages. For example, the loss being compensated must not be too remote from the actual wrong. Also, the person who suffers the loss has a duty to **mitigate** that loss. This means they must do what they can to avoid or minimise the extent of the loss.

The time of assessment of damages can be relevant, too. Generally, damages are calculated at a value as at the time of the wrong. Interest may also be available, calculated at a rate set by the court.

Equity is a source of remedies developed over the centuries, to prevent general injustice within the legal system. Equitable remedies are not always available and can be quite technical, but they form an important part of Australian law and have figured in many of our major cases. The most useful are specific performance, declaration and the injunction:

- **specific performance** orders a party to a contract to perform that contract;
- a **declaration** sets out the final state of affairs between the parties. A good example of this is a declaration that a debt is not owed;
- an **injunction** orders certain behaviour. It can require a party to do a certain act or it can restrain a party from doing a certain act. For example, when a claim is lodged at a court, between the time

a claim is lodged and the date of the hearing, in certain circumstances it may be possible for an injunction to be applied for and granted to prevent a party from carrying out the offending behaviour until the case can be heard.

For administrative law, that is the law concerning the review of government decisions, legislation now largely regulates the remedies available. However, where there is a shortfall in redressing a wrong or holding an official accountable, a group of remedies called **prerogative writs** may still be granted.

Mandamus is a prerogative writ that means 'we order'. It orders a public official to carry out their public duty or else give reasons to the court for not doing so.

Prohibition is an order that forbids the public official from doing a certain act.

Certiorari orders an inferior court or tribunal or administrative body to produce a written record of proceedings to be reviewed by a higher court.

Most cases that come before our courts and tribunals involve remedies that are quite straightforward and are spelt out clearly in the legislation or the agreement made between the parties. As you progress through this book, if you are not sure of the remedies for your case or if you think there may be others available, be sure to get legal advice.

8
The litigation process

There are exceptions, but most non-criminal litigation roughly follows this simple pattern:

CLAIM then DEFENCE then CONFERENCE then HEARING then RESULT

First, a party called the plaintiff or applicant or claimant starts proceedings by lodging an application or claim at the registry of the court or tribunal and paying a **filing fee.**

Next, a copy of the claim is issued to the other party. The other party is called the respondent or defendant. Once the claim is issued, the respondent has the opportunity to respond to it within a certain time by lodging a written defence. Once the defence is lodged a copy of it is then forwarded to the plaintiff.

Although in some instances a case can proceed without a written defence, usually if no defence is lodged within the specified time, the plaintiff can proceed quickly and have the case dealt with at this early stage by applying for judgment. This is called **default judgment.**

If a defence is lodged within time, the next stage of the case is often a meeting between the parties arranged by the court or tribunal. There are various names for this meeting, such as **preliminary conference** or **case management conference** or **mediation.** Its purpose is to clarify the issues in the case and explore any options for settling the dispute without it going to a hearing. At the conference, the parties meet with an official of the court or tribunal and discuss the case. If they find a solution, the terms of settlement are drawn up and signed by the parties and the matter ends there. Or there may be further steps arranged towards a settlement on mutually agreed terms. If the case does not settle at this conference and the parties are no closer to a resolution, a hearing date will be set.

If it does not settle but isn't yet ready for a hearing because more preparations must be made, often a minor hearing date will be set. This is called a **directions hearing.** For example, more evidence may need to be collected, more documentation completed or the availability of a witness confirmed. At the directions hearing, the court or tribunal issues directions about what must be done to ensure that all preparations are completed before the final hearing date. There are other versions of preliminary hearings, called **call-overs** and **mentions** that deal with setting dates, completing arrangements, dealing with adjournments and generally keeping a case moving forward.

In the early stages of a case, the court or tribunal is sometimes asked by a party to grant preliminary orders that operate until the main hearing takes place. These are called **interim orders** or **interlocutory orders.** The applications for these orders can be complex.

At the final or main hearing, the case is heard in its entirety, with each party having the opportunity to present its case and reply to the other party's case. The party making the claim – the plaintiff – goes first in presenting their case.

The burden of proof, that is, the obligation to prove the case, is on the party who is making the claim. If it is not adequately proved, the claim fails and, in effect, the party defending the claim – the respondent – has won.

The test used for the burden of proof in non-criminal cases, to determine whether the plaintiff has adequately proved their case, is the **balance of probabilities.** This test isn't as tough as the one used for criminal cases. It means that the plaintiff's case doesn't have to be proved beyond reasonable doubt, but rather that it is more probable than not.

The result or decision might be given verbally at the end of the hearing or else is **reserved,** that is, made available at a later date. A written copy of the decision or the orders that are made is usually made available immediately or sent to the parties soon after.

Most decisions can be appealed to a higher body, but there are often strict guidelines for appealing and strict time limits apply.

9
The golden rules of litigation

Success in litigation depends on three things: the facts, the law and the presentation; that is:

1. how strong and reliable your evidence is to establish the facts;
2. whether the law can be used in your favour;
3. how clearly and coherently you present your case.

To make the most of these three ingredients for success there are some important rules, learnt the hard way by our country's best and worst litigation lawyers. Throughout this book you will be reminded of them. As you'll see, to use them you don't need a law degree. Here they are:

THE GOLDEN RULES

THE DOs

DO YOUR HOMEWORK; BE PREPARED
KEEP ACCURATE RECORDS
OBEY THE TIME LIMITS FOR LODGING DOCUMENTS
KNOW THE FACTS
CONFIRM THE FACTS WITH EVIDENCE
KNOW THE LAW
KNOW HOW THE LAW APPLIES TO THE FACTS
GET RID OF YOUR EMOTION
CONDUCT YOURSELF POLITELY AND PROFESSIONALLY
IF YOU GET SIDETRACKED, DON'T LOSE YOUR WAY
BE SIMPLE, BE BRIEF
EXPECT SURPRISES

THE DON'Ts

DON'T BE AFRAID TO ASK QUESTIONS
DON'T WASTE TIME ON IRRELEVANCIES
DON'T GET RATTLED, DON'T BE BULLDOZED
NEVER FORGET WHAT YOU WANT

10

Preparing your case part 1

There are many ways to prepare a case. What follows is one practical method that gives you the information you need while at the same time building your skills. It is divided into three parts.

This chapter deals with the early stages of litigation; that is, the preparation of the claim, the defence and the conference. Use this chapter in conjunction with chapter 11 to understand the requirements of these early stages of your litigation while you are collecting your evidence and researching the law.

The claim

The claim must be accurate and complete, and contain sufficient information to enable you to establish your case at the hearing. If it lacks

10

Preparing your case part 1

There are many ways to prepare a case. What follows is one practical method that gives you the information you need while at the same time building your skills. It is divided into three parts.

This chapter deals with the early stages of litigation; that is, the preparation of the claim, the defence and the conference. Use this chapter in conjunction with chapter 11 to understand the requirements of these early stages of your litigation while you are collecting your evidence and researching the law.

The claim

The claim must be accurate and complete and contain sufficient information to enable you to establish your case at the hearing. If it misses important elements or details it may be difficult to raise them later and you could lose your case unnecessarily. The better the claim, the more likely you will settle the case at an early stage or win at the hearing.

To make an application or claim, you first need to know where, what and how to claim. Use the services already mentioned in chapter 6 'Where to go for help' for the necessary information and advice. Check also with the registry of the court or tribunal and with any brochures, fact sheets or information kits available about lodging a claim.

The claim can usually be started in the state or territory where you or the other party live or where the dispute occurred. Under certain circumstances it can be transferred elsewhere.

There may be strict time limits for commencing your legal action. This is called its **limitation date** or **limitation period** and is usually measured in years or months from the date the cause of the action arose. It may be as much as five or seven years or as little as six months and can prevent you from lodging a claim if you leave it too late.

If you suspect that your dispute may be out of time to make a claim, get legal advice immediately about the limitation date.

Sometimes, but not often, you may have a choice of where to start the claim, for example a local court or a specialist tribunal. Although tribunals tend to be informal and less costly, get advice about the best choice for your case.

Be sure that the court or tribunal you use is the right one. Check with the website or registry that it has the **jurisdiction,** or powers, to deal with your kind of dispute and to give you the remedy you are seeking.

CASE STUDY MURRAY'S BOARDER

When Murray's lodger finally moved out, she left behind a legacy of unpaid rent along with bills for her share of the electricity and telephone and a vandalised bedroom. To Murray's surprise, he discovered he couldn't pursue the debt in the local Tenancy Tribunal, as technically a lodger isn't a tenant. Luckily, Murray

> checked with the tribunal before lodging the claim and was advised to use the Small Claims Court instead. As his claim was for under $10 000, which was the allowable money limit for the Small Claims Court, Murray lodged his claim without a hitch and saved himself the wasted time and effort of a wrong claim in a wrong court.

Be sure too that you have the correct details of the other party, especially their right name and right address. Check your records and update any changes in details. An error with this simple information can result in lengthy delays or your claim being rejected.

{*Golden Rule of Litigation:* **KEEP ACCURATE RECORDS**}

There are various names for the claim, depending on the type of case and the particular court or tribunal involved. It might be called an **application** or a **statement of claim,** an ordinary or special claim, a claim for liquidated damages or perhaps some other name. If it is an appeal of a government decision it might be called an **application for review.**

With some claims you need only to provide the parties' details, a brief explanation of the problem and the amount of money being claimed or the order being sought. With others you might need to set out all the material facts necessary to establish your case. If your application is an appeal against a government decision, you will need to give details of the government decision and an explanation of why you think the decision is wrong. You might also need to attach a copy of the government decision as well as any documents that support your explanation.

The claim may be a simple form with clear questions about the information that's required. Or it may be a specific format legal document that you must draft yourself. Other legal documents might also need to be included with the claim. A Family Law claim, for instance, may need to be accompanied by an **affidavit.** Chapter

11 helps you with drafting legal documents.

If the claim is a form that you fill out, you may need to pick up the form from the registry of the court or tribunal or have it posted to you. Or else you may be able to complete and lodge it online, or download it and fill out a printed copy and lodge it manually. In any event, you must read the form very carefully. Make sure you comply with any requirements, for instance about the use of black ink, block letters and ruling out empty spaces on the form. If you are lodging an online application, be sure you make the correct selections and enter all details accurately.

Before filling out the claim or completing it online, follow these important steps:

Compile a **chronology** of your dispute, listing the relevant events in date order. This will help you pinpoint relevant facts and dates and simplify the dispute in your mind.

Research the available remedies for your case and determine exactly what it is you want to claim. Be specific: what outcomes do you want from the decision-maker? It might be a sum of money. Or it might be an order ending or varying an agreement. It might be an order giving you certain rights, like a parenting order concerning your children. The order might contain certain conditions. Or, if you are appealing a government decision you may want the decision set aside.

Check on the claim form or at the website or with registry staff what else can be claimed. For example, can you claim the cost of the filing fee? Can you claim interest? If so, from what date and at what rate? If you're on a low income, check whether the filing fee can be waived; that is, whether you can be exempt from paying it.

Next, look at the legal requirements of your case and make a list of the legal elements necessary to establish your claim. These include the relevant sections of applicable legislation and, if the case involves an agreement made between the parties, the terms and conditions of this agreement. It may also include relevant cases. Use chapter 6 'Where to go for help' to obtain legal advice and chapter 11 'Preparing your case part 2' for researching the law.

From the chronology make a list of the relevant facts and, alongside each fact, list in brackets the evidence you have or will need to confirm the fact. You will need evidence to verify the basic facts of the case as well as any fact that is in dispute and that you need to establish your case. For evidence that you need but don't have, set about collecting it as soon as possible. Chapter 11 will help you with collecting your evidence. From this list, mark down on your list of legal requirements which facts, with which evidence, fulfil which legal requirements.

If you are aware of the substance of the other party's case, also make a list of its elements. Exactly what are they contesting? Do they have a different version of the facts? If so, what evidence are they using to support this? Are they claiming that the facts don't satisfy the legal requirements? Are they interpreting the law differently?

Using your lists, now outline the argument of your case, explaining why you should get what you want. Set out the law and the facts and show how the facts, as confirmed by your evidence, fulfil the legal requirements and thereby establish your claim.

Also, include in your argument reasons why the other party's case should fail. For example, the evidence or the law doesn't support their case, their evidence is inadequate to prove their facts, your evidence is better than theirs. Give details.

Now, briefly summarise your case in three or four sentences.

Finally, express your case in a nutshell. In one or two sentences, what are the issues? What is its essence?

Opposite is a simple example to get you started.

These steps take considerable time and energy, but they are vital. In chapter 12 'Preparing your case part 3' you will build on these lists to form an outline for your presentation at the hearing. Put the effort into these lists now and you'll find your case will become manageable and easier than you expected.

Use the information you have compiled so far to assess whether your claim is a valid one and to identify its strengths and weaknesses. This will assist you to separate your feelings of grievance from the legal matters. If your case is a poor one or you think you may have no case at all, get legal advice to confirm this. It's much better to discover now rather than later if your claim has no chance. Should you proceed, you would risk having costs awarded against you.

CASE STUDY JED'S DEBT CLAIM

Jed had an agreement with a builder to renovate his back verandah. He paid the first instalment for materials but the builder never returned to start the work. Now he wants his money back.

His chronology would include the date he contacted and negotiated with the builder, the date they both signed the agreement, the date he paid the money and the dates of any attempts he made to contact the builder as well as the date of any letter of demand he sent.

Jed has researched the appropriate tribunal that will deal with his claim and the remedies available. He wants a refund of his money plus the cost of lodging the claim plus interest calculated according to the rate fixed by the tribunal.

The legal requirements of Jed's claim are the clauses of the agreement that relate to the responsibilities of the builder to do the work within a specified time, and also clauses relating to any breach of the agreement. The requirements also include provisions of relevant legislation relating to this type of agreement. In Jed's state, the consumer legislation allows the particular tribunal to make an order for the refund of his money plus the cost of the filing fee plus interest.

Jed's list of facts and evidence would include the actual agreement and the date it was signed, any plans prepared for the work, details of the payment Jed made to the builder (including receipts), printouts of any emails he sent the builder asking him to get started on the work, photographs of the verandah and copies of any letters he sent the builder, including the letter of demand.

As far as Jed knows, the substance of the builder's case seems to be, 'yeah, yeah, I'll get to it'. That is, no case.

The argument for Jed's case is:
- the parties signed an agreement on 10 June 2008. Under clause 4 of that agreement Jed would pay four instalments of $4000. Under clause 2 the builder would renovate the verandah according to the plans. According to clause 6 the builder would start work within six weeks of the first instalment and would complete the work within two months of the start date. Clause 15 of the written agreement provides for a full refund of the money where the builder breaches clause 6;
- on the same day Jed paid the builder $4000 and received a receipt;
- it is now October and, as the photographs show, no work has begun;

- under section 21 of the *Consumer Act* the consumer tribunal has power to order a refund of money plus the filing fee plus interest;
- under the clauses of the contract, Jed is clearly entitled to a refund of his money;
- Jed has tried contacting the builder on a number of occasions and received no reply to his letter of demand. The builder has provided no reasons for his breach and has made no attempt to rectify the situation.

A summary of Jed's case would be that he entered an agreement with a builder to renovate his verandah and paid the first instalment of $4000. The agreement entitled Jed to a return of his money if the work wasn't started within six weeks after the payment. The work was never started.

In a nutshell, Jed paid $4000 and signed an agreement, which was breached. The clauses of the agreement entitle Jed to the return of his money.

CASE STUDY ROBBIE GETS REAL

Robbie was missing his children terribly. He had originally agreed with his ex-wife to flexible arrangements regarding the children. Things seemed to work well at first with the children spending alternate weekends with Robbie.

Now 12 months down the track, Robbie was often missing out. He was doing all the right things, but there was always a problem when he rang about picking up the kids. At first he was agreeable if it didn't suit his ex-wife's other arrangements. But Robbie couldn't help feeling his ex-wife was making life difficult for him and he was seeing his children less and less.

Robbie wanted to apply to the Family Court to have the matter sorted out and the alternate weekend arrangement formalised. At first he felt uncertain about whether he would be successful and he wasn't confident at all about taking the matter to court.

After getting some legal advice and examining what he could offer his children, Robbie decided that he wanted to and could provide more than just alternate weekends. He had changed jobs recently and was no longer travelling regularly. His new home had plenty of room for the children and his mother lived nearby and was active in their lives.

Robbie applied to the Family Court to have his dispute regarding the children mediated. When this was not successful, Robbie proceeded to have the matter heard by the court. He asked for an order giving him every weekend with the children as well as special occasions and half the school holidays.

Instead of settling for fighting for alternate weekends, Robbie was changing the dispute into a claim for what he was needing. Robbie went ahead with the application, provided appropriate evidence of his changed circumstances, and at the hearing Robbie got what he asked for.

Once you are confident you have a case, check from your research whether the remedy you're seeking is justified. Do you have legitimate grounds for claiming what you're claiming?

Now realistically assess whether you can ask for more as Robbie did in the case study on the previous page. Ask yourself again, what fair result can you seek in order to feel satisfied. Remember, you won't get what you don't ask for.

Now draft your claim from your lists. Make it straightforward and clear. Be sure to include all the requirements and, if you're claiming a sum of money, include all the amounts of money you're claiming and can claim, and itemise each amount. Check that your calculations are correct.

Check on the claim form or at the website or with registry staff how many extra copies of the claim you must provide when you **file** the claim; that is, when you lodge it. Often three are needed because once they're stamped, one is given back to you, one is kept by the registry for use by the court or tribunal, and one is for the other party.

Check also whether the registry will serve the copy on the other party or whether you must attend to that. If it is your job, check whether posting it or faxing it is allowed or whether it has to be served in person.

If you wish to change or add to your claim or application after you have lodged it, you may need to prepare a new amended version and necessary copies, to be lodged and provided to the court or tribunal and the other party. Depending on the stage your case has reached, you may need to get permission from the court or tribunal to lodge an amended claim or else agreement from the other party. Check with the registry or the website of the court or tribunal.

STEPS FOR PREPARING THE CLAIM
- prepare a chronology;
- determine exactly what you will claim;
- list the legal requirements necessary to establish your claim;

- list the relevant facts then list the evidence you have or can get to confirm the facts;
- on the list of legal requirements, mark down which facts, with which evidence, fulfil the requirements;
- list the elements of the other party's case;
- using your lists and by applying the facts to the law, outline the arguments of your case. Include why the other party's case should fail;
- summarise your case in three or four sentences;
- condense the summary to one or two sentences. What is your case, in a nutshell?

CHECKLIST FOR PREPARING THE CLAIM

- is your claim accurate and complete? Does it contain sufficient information to enable you to establish your case at the hearing?
- are the details of the other party correct?
- is it within its limitation period?

- does the court or tribunal you are using have the jurisdiction to deal with your kind of dispute?
- can you claim the cost of the filing fee? Can you claim interest? If so, at what rate and for what period? Is waiver of the filing fee available?
- are your money calculations correct?
- do you need to include other documents with your claim, for example, an affidavit?
- do you need to lodge extra copies of the claim? If so, how many?
- do you need to serve the claim on the other party?

The defence

If you have received a claim against you, the first rule is don't panic.

The next rule is the same as the first. Calm down.

There's no point taking this claim personally. Really, it is just business. Whether it's family law, an insurance claim, neighbourhood dispute or some other civil matter, it is just the business of people adjusting their legal entitlements against one another. Being angry or upset about it isn't productive. It will damage your ability to fight the claim systematically.

{***Golden Rule of Litigation:*** GET RID OF THE EMOTION}

Next, examine the claim very carefully. What exactly do they want? What exactly are they asserting? How do they intend to justify it?

Remember that the pressure is on the other party, the plaintiff, to prove their case, not on you. After all, they have issued the claim. So they must back it up adequately and if they cannot, the claim fails. The only pressure that is on you as respondent is to show how the plaintiff's case is not adequately established.

The claim will contain important information for you about what to do next and how to do it. For example, if the claim is in a higher court or tribunal like the Supreme Court you may need to **enter an appearance.** This is a form you lodge within a specified time. It acknowledges that you are the respondent and gives your address for service of documents.

The claim will also give you a time limit for lodging your defence. If you wish to defend the matter, be sure to obey this time limit. If you don't lodge your defence in time you run the risk of the plaintiff applying for **default judgment** against you, and without further warning or chance to respond, you may find yourself being held liable for the claim.

If this happens to you and you have good reason for not lodging the defence in time, you may be able to apply to have the judgment set aside and then continue with lodging your defence. But be warned: courts and tribunals do not take kindly to applications of this type and will not grant them except for the most compelling reasons.

{*Golden Rule of Litigation:* OBEY THE TIME LIMITS FOR LODGING DOCUMENTS}

The defence is your formal response to the claim. It notifies the other party and the court or tribunal that you are challenging the claim. If you put the time and effort in now to construct a strong defence, your case will proceed more smoothly and your chances of success will improve. If you miss important issues or details, it may be difficult or useless to try to raise them later on. Also, the better and more complete your defence, the more likely your opponent will withdraw the claim or try to settle the case out of court.

To begin preparing your defence you will need to compile a number of lists. These lists will form the nuts and bolts of your defence, so attend to them thoroughly. They will also be used later in chapter 12 'Preparing your case part 3' to form the outline for your presentation at the hearing.

First, prepare a chronology of the dispute listing all the relevant events in date order. This will show you the dispute in its entirety and expose any gaps or inconsistencies between the other party's claim and your version of the events.

Your defence must address the claim. So next, make a list of the elements of the claim. This will help you analyse and understand the claim, especially if it's confusing or long-winded.

If you have difficulty understanding exactly what the claim is about because it is pleaded in a short or abbreviated form or it is incomplete or doesn't contain enough factual information, write as soon as possible to the other party or their lawyer requesting **further and better particulars** of the claim so that you can address the claim properly in your defence. Be specific about the information you are requesting: for example, additional information about a specific aspect of the claim, copies of documents that you don't have that relate to the claim, or details of how the amounts in the claim were calculated. Give a time frame for complying with the request, for example 14 days, and be sure to sign and date the letter and keep a copy for your records.

A letter requesting further and better particulars from the other party may affect the time limit for lodging your defence. Notify the court or tribunal of your request and check regarding the time limit.

Next, get legal advice using chapter 6 'Where to go for help' and do research using the section on 'Legal research' in chapter 11 'Preparing your case part 2', to find out and list the legal requirements of the claim. Identify exactly what the plaintiff must fulfil, legally, to succeed in their case. If the claim involves an agreement made between the parties, the legal requirements will include not only the applicable legislation but also the terms and conditions of that agreement.

Now go through the claim and make a list of all the points in the claim that you challenge. For example, some of the crucial facts might be wrong or missing. Perhaps one or some of the legal requirements have been ignored. Perhaps the law doesn't support the plaintiff's claim in the way that they say it does. If the claim is for money, check that the amounts are itemised. Are they added up correctly? Are the amounts actually claimable? If not, add it to your list.

Using your chronology and any other information you may have, mark on your list of challenges to the claim beside the relevant points any facts you have to support these points, then itemise what evidence you have or can get to verify them. Things like photographs, invoices, quotations, receipts, letters, clauses of the contract, the lease, or the testimony of witnesses are just some forms of evidence you can use to confirm your facts. Chapter 11 will help you with the facts and the evidence. Set about collecting your evidence as soon as possible.

Next, consider carefully what concrete outcome do you want from this case? Be specific: what outcomes do you want from the decision-maker? Do you want the plaintiff's claim dismissed? Do you want the court or tribunal to make some other specific order? If the claim is for an amount of money, do you want the amount reduced? Do you want to make a claim yourself? Exactly what will mark a satisfactory result for you?

Perhaps you want more than just to defeat the claim. You might find that in defending the claim you can, for the first time, ask for what you've needed all along to finally put this dispute to rest. If so, get legal advice and do research on what other action may be available for your case so that you can make the most of this opportunity in your defence.

As part of your defence to the claim, or in addition to it, you might want to make a claim yourself against the plaintiff. This is called either a **cross-claim** or **counter claim,** depending on whether you are denying their claim completely and making your own claim, or whether you're admitting liability for the claim but asking that the amount claimed be offset by the amount you are now claiming.

Simply speaking, in a cross-claim for example, you might be saying 'no, I am not liable for the $3000 you are claiming, in fact, in this dispute you are liable for $2000'. In a counter claim you might be saying 'yes, I'm liable for that $3000, but in this dispute you also owe me $2000, so I am only liable for a total of $1000'.

Your cross- or counter claim against the plaintiff may not have to relate to the same dispute. It may be able to relate to a different set of facts or a completely different complaint. Check with the court or tribunal about the rules for this.

CASE STUDY THANH GETS CREATIVE

Thanh was defending a Family Court application by his ex-wife to have his contact hours with his children reduced. The application was based on allegations about him that were untrue.

At first Thanh felt ill-prepared and on the defensive. He didn't know where to start to defend this claim, he had no lawyer and his previous encounters with the Family court had been a disaster.

Through a local support group for divorced fathers, Thanh got some telephone numbers and rang around for the help he needed. He was able to get some one-off legal advice about his problem and took the time to consider his situation very carefully. He could see a way to prove the allegations to be untrue, but he also looked at what he wanted for his

> children and what he could reasonably provide for them.
>
> Thanh got the evidence he needed and went ahead with his defence, but in it he included an application of his own for the contact arrangements to be varied in a way that suited him better.

Although a cross- or counter claim can effectively change the nature of a dispute, it must have a valid basis. You must be able to substantiate your cross- or counter claim, just as the plaintiff must be able to substantiate their claim.

You might be able to include the cross- or counter claim as part of your written defence or you might be required to lodge a separate document or form, attracting a filing fee. Check with the website or registry of the court or tribunal. If there is a fee for the cross- or counter claim and you're on a low income, check whether you can get **waiver;** that is, exemption from paying the fee.

Once you have identified exactly what result you want, return to your lists and using all the information you have compiled so far – that is, the elements of the claim, the legal requirements, the points that challenge the claim and your facts and evidence – set out in detail your argument as to why the plaintiff's case should fail.

Next, prepare a brief summary of your case in three or four sentences. Then condense this further into one or two sentences. What is your case, in a nutshell?

Here is one example of these lists for a defence:

CASE STUDY KIM'S CURTAINS

Kim and her mum had a successful curtain business with many years' experience between them. They obtained most of their customers through word of mouth and rarely had complaints. Any problem was always fixed promptly and courteously and they prided themselves on their attention to detail and their customer service.

To their great frustration and against their advice, one customer insisted on using fabric she had that was well known to fade. Kim and her mum still made the curtains, but they used a style that when open, would minimise their exposure to the afternoon sun. They gave specific instructions about the care of these curtains and the customer assured them that in the daytime they would always be open. When the curtains were hung, the customer was very pleased with the job.

Eighteen months later, without warning and with a rude note attached, the curtains were returned in poor condition with substantial fading. Shortly after, Kim received a consumer tribunal claim by the customer for the cost of replacing the curtains.

To defend the claim, Kim's chronology would include the dates she and her mum attended the customer's home to advise and quote on the curtains, the date the quote was accepted, the date they delivered and hung the curtains and the date they were paid. It would include the specific dates they advised of the risk of fading, advised of the choice of style and the date they gave instructions about their care.

The claim alleged that Kim and her mum hadn't made the curtains properly, and due to the fading they were no longer fit for their purpose. The elements of the claim were that Kim and her mum had breached implied conditions in the agreement that they made with the customer to make and install the curtains. The alleged breaches were:

- they had not exercised due care and skill;
- the curtains were not of merchantable quality;
- they were now not fit for their purpose.

Kim got legal advice and researched the law in her state. In her list of legal requirements she put the specific provisions of her state's *Fair Trading Act and Consumer Claims Act* concerning the implied conditions and also the factors the tribunal must take into account when making orders regarding a consumer claim. Kim even found a case of the tribunal's that was similar and was decided in the curtain maker's favour. The case showed that the test for any breach of the implied conditions is an objective assessment of the respondent's (that is, the curtain maker's) conduct: did the curtain maker act in a reasonable manner that accords with the skills ordinarily expected of a person in this field; and were the curtains of a reasonable quality, taking into account their purpose, price and any other relevant matter. Kim included this case in her list.

Her points of challenge to the claim involved all of the alleged breaches. She felt sure that she and her mum had acted in a reasonable manner and exercised due skill and care in making and installing the curtains; that the curtains were of merchantable quality; and that, with the style used and the advice and instructions about their care, they were fit for the purpose.

Beside the points of challenge, Kim listed the important facts and evidence she had to refute the elements of the claim. She had a copy of the quote given to the customer. Against the item marked 'material to be used' it stated 'Customer's fabric. May fade.' Her mum's hand-drawn design for the curtains accompanying the quote also showed arrows for opening and closing with the words 'to reduce fading' beside the arrows. Kim's copy of their invoice also included instructions for the care of the curtains.

The curtains themselves would be good evidence for Kim's case as the particular faded areas showed the style had been tampered with, producing prolonged exposure to strong sun. Kim's mum also set to making a small, portable version of the curtain with the same curtain tracks and rings and style of curtain to show how the style worked, if properly used, to protect the fabric.

For her facts and evidence Kim would include her own and her mum's testimony.

The remedy Kim wanted for the case was to have the customer's case dismissed.

In her argument section Kim used the quotation, the invoice, the curtains themselves, her mum's miniature replica and her and her mum's own testimony to argue that, by first advising against using that fabric, by using a suitable style to minimise the risk of fading and by making and installing the curtains to the customer's own satisfaction with appropriate instructions about their care having regard to the risk, she and her mum had acted reasonably and had not breached the implied terms of the agreement. They were therefore not liable for the cost of replacing the curtains.

Kim's summary was that she and her mum were not liable for replacing the curtains because they had not breached the implied conditions of their agreement with the customer. They had exercised due skill and care in the making and installation of the curtains and the curtains, when made

> and installed, were of merchantable quality and fit for their purpose.
>
> In a nutshell, Kim and her mum are not liable to replace the curtains because they have not breached the agreement.

Finally, return to your list of points that challenge the claim and assess whether your defence is a valid one. Do your challenges have substance? Do they actually attack the heart of the matter, the crucial elements of the claim, or do they just pick away at the edges? It will be no use pointing to errors in the other party's case if these errors are largely irrelevant to the substance of the claim. While you're busy picking at the lies and inconsistencies of who said what and when, if they don't relate to defeating the elements, the other party will still establish their claim and you will be found liable.

At this or any other stage of the proceedings you can contact the other party or their lawyer and offer to settle, or end, the matter. To negotiate a settlement, do it in writing and clearly title the letter **'Without Prejudice'**. This means the offer to settle is given without it prejudicing your case in any way. It prevents the other party from using the letter against you in court later on if the matter doesn't settle.

One school of thought says the letter should be marked 'Without Prejudice Save as to Costs'. This means that if the matter doesn't settle, you the letter writer can still tender it in court on an argument about costs. For example, you offer to settle for X amount and the offer is rejected and the matter goes to court. If the court result is similar to what you offered your opponent in the first place, then when your opponent asks the court for an order that you pay the legal costs, you can use this letter to argue against such an order. After all, if the offer had been accepted, it would have saved the court's time and the legal costs.

Don't forget to sign and date the letter and keep a copy. Negotiations to settle a case do not stop the court process, so keep an eye on the time limit for lodging your defence. If the matter does settle, notify the court or tribunal. You may need to sign consent orders or other forms to finalise the litigation.

Whether or not you want to settle the case, the clock for your defence is still ticking, so get started now on drafting your defence. Use your lists.

There may be a particular format for the defence or a particular form that must be used. It might have a special name like 'Response' or 'Statement Contesting the Application' or it might also have a number like 'Form 9'. You may be able to fill out and lodge a defence form online or else download it and print it, fill it in and lodge it yourself.

For information about the form or format of the defence, check on the claim itself or at the website or registry of the court or tribunal. Make the most of any brochures, fact sheets or information kits available from the registry about defending a claim.

The requirements of the defence and its degree of formality vary depending on the nature of the claim and the court or tribunal involved. You might need to address each paragraph of the claim stating whether you agree or disagree with it. This helps clarify the issues and narrow the dispute. If you neither agree nor disagree with a particular paragraph you can say so. Use your lists to help you.

Or you might be required to just state briefly why you oppose the claim. Again, use your lists. You might also be asked whether you are seeking other orders yourself.

There may be a filing fee for lodging your defence. Check with the website or registry and check if waiver is available. Check also whether you need to provide extra copies of your defence when you lodge it. For example you may need the original plus two copies. One copy (when stamped by the registry) will be returned to you, one is for the plaintiff and the original is kept for use by the court or tribunal.

Check too whether, after the defence is lodged, the court or tribunal will **serve** it on the plaintiff, that is, provide it to the plaintiff, or whether you must attend to this. If it's you, ask if posting or faxing is allowed.

If at a later stage you wish to change your defence or add to it, you will need to prepare an **amended defence** and lodge it with the registry. In some instances you may need to get permission first. Check with the registry. Check also if you need to provide extra copies and whether they or you will serve it on the plaintiff.

If you are the applicant in an appeal against the decision of a government department, the department's response is not called a defence. Instead, the department must give to the court or tribunal, within a specified time, a copy of all the relevant documents used in making the original decision. These documents show exactly what the department's case entails and often include a statement setting out the reasons for the decision. They may be called **T docs** or Tribunal Documents. The court or tribunal will send you a copy of these as soon as they receive them.

STEPS FOR PREPARING THE DEFENCE
- Examine the claim carefully;

- Prepare a chronology;
- List the elements of the claim;
- List the legal requirements of the claim;
- List your points of challenge to the claim. Mark on it any facts you have to support your challenge. Beside those facts, itemise what evidence you have or can get to support those facts;
- Determine the outcome you want from the case;
- If you wish to cross- or counter claim, obtain advice and research the requirements. Follow the steps for preparing a claim;
- Using your lists, set out your argument for the case, explaining how and why the other party's case should fail;
- Briefly summarise your case in three or four sentences;
- Reduce it to one or two sentences. What is your case, in a nutshell?

CHECKLIST FOR THE DEFENCE
- Is your defence clear and accurate?

- Does it address the elements of the claim?
- If you need more details of the claim, have you written requesting further and better particulars?
- Are you lodging the defence in time?
- Do you need to include other documents with the defence?
- Is there a filing fee for the defence? Is waiver available?
- Do you need to lodge extra copies of the defence?
- Do you need to serve it on the other party?

The conference

The case conference, or mediation as it is sometimes called, is a fairly new addition to the litigation process. Not all courts and tribunals use it. Its aim is to save the court's or tribunal's time and expense by filtering out the cases that should settle without going to a hearing and by progressing those that will go to the hearing stage.

The conference is a meeting attended by both parties and/or their lawyers, with an official of the court or tribunal presiding over it. The official's job is not to take sides or adjudicate on the case but to facilitate a productive meeting between the parties.

It might take place at the court or tribunal or by telephone link-up. It is informal and any discussions of the issues take place on a without prejudice basis. This means that these discussions can't be used as evidence against you later on at the hearing.

The conference gives the parties the chance to explore the issues, identify the strengths and weaknesses of each other's case and explore any options for compromise. It's an opportunity for each side to learn more about the other's case, to clarify points of agreement and disagreement, discuss the facts and the law and pursue any queries about evidence. If the evidence of witnesses will be used in the case, you can use the conference to notify the other party which of their witnesses will need to attend the hearing so that you can cross-examine them.

At the conference you can also ask the official any questions about process or the next steps to the hearing. Although they won't give legal advice, they can help you with valuable, practical tips.

Some conferences resemble barnyard squabbles, with the parties becoming very emotional. This wastes everybody's time as it usually accomplishes very little. Even worse, it distracts you from the issues of your case that you must confront if you wish to succeed. It's important to set aside your sense of grievance and focus on the legal matters you are trying to resolve.

Try to use this meeting strategically. Take your paperwork with you as well as any documents that could help clarify or resolve the matter. Beforehand, try to understand which points you and your opponent agree on and which ones you don't, so you can work on these at the conference. Also try to pinpoint any areas of compromise that you're willing to negotiate. And beforehand, know your fall-back position and your ultimate bottom line in this case.

During the conference be prepared to be constructive and co-operative, but have your wits about you. Your opponent may appeal to your hip pocket, your values or your ego without necessarily offering anything of substance or genuine compromise. So don't allow yourself to be sweet-talked or bulldozed into a position that doesn't serve your interests. Take time to consider the pros and cons of any proposal carefully before agreeing to it.

{***Golden Rule of Litigation:*** DON'T GET RATTLED, DON'T BE BULLDOZED}

A successful conference may or may not result in settling the case, but it should certainly help progress it. Use it to learn as much as you can about the other party's case so that you can better assess the merits of their case as well as your own.

If the conference results in the parties agreeing to settle the case, they can draw up an agreement with the court or tribunal official and sign it then and there. If the agreement is complied with, the settlement is then formalised and the legal proceedings are ended.

If the case doesn't get resolved, usually at the end of the conference, a hearing date is set. In some jurisdictions further conferences can be held.

If the conference process doesn't result in settling the case, you must now begin preparing for the hearing.

CASE STUDY CONFERENCES

In Conference Room 1 of the Tribunal, Tribunal Member Smith is pleased with the progress the parties are making in sorting out the issues of their case. They have worked out what they agree on and have moved on to discussing what they cannot agree on.

Next door in Conference Room 2, Tribunal Member Cooper and the parties at least agree on one thing: that this case won't settle and must go to a hearing. They have systematically gone through the elements of the claim and defence, and are now busy discussing evidence.

Across the hall in Conference Room 3, Tribunal Member Tsakis is having a much harder time. The parties are bickering terribly and it is starting to get personal. Ms Tsakis repeatedly tries to return them to the issues, but now with only 15 minutes to go in the 45-minute conference, she isn't hopeful.

Back in Conference Room 1, the parties don't settle their case, but they do come up with a mutually agreeable plan. If the plaintiff provides the requested evidence within the next week, the respondent will pay two-thirds of the amount claimed. The plaintiff will then contact the Tribunal and withdraw the claim. Tribunal Member Smith agrees to review the file in fortnight's time and, if the case has not settled, he will set a hearing date. The parties leave the conference, satisfied that their time has been well spent.

In Conference Room 2, the parties have narrowed the issues that are in contention and indicated which of the other party's witnesses will be needed for cross-examination at the hearing. With no other preparations to be finalised, Tribunal Member Cooper sets a hearing date and they pack up their paperwork and leave.

In Conference Room 3, the conference has gone over time and no progress has been made at all. The issues are no clearer, there has been no discussion of the evidence and the parties have gained nothing that helps their case. They are disgruntled and exhausted. Tribunal Member Tsakis is unable to offer them another conference. She sets a hearing date for the case and the parties leave the conference angrier than ever.

11

Preparing your case part 2

Preparing your case for a hearing involves a number of steps. This chapter deals with collecting your evidence to prove the facts and researching the law that applies to your case. It includes information about different forms of evidence as well as some basics about legal processes, documents and the jargon. These matters are the nuts and bolts of litigation.

The decision-maker's first job at the hearing will be to determine what the facts of the case are, then to determine which law or laws apply. Then the decision-maker will apply that law to those facts in order to see whether the plaintiff has a case and whether the plaintiff has adequately proved that case.

The test of proof the decision-maker will use is the balance of probabilities. With this test, the plaintiff doesn't have to prove their case beyond reasonable doubt but must prove that it is more probable than not. And the **burden of proof** is on the plaintiff. This means that the obligation to prove the case is on the plaintiff. Regardless of what the respondent does or doesn't do, if the plaintiff doesn't sufficiently establish their case, then the claim fails and is dismissed. End of story.

The plaintiff's goal at the hearing, then, is to prove their case; that is, their version of the facts and interpretation of the law, on the balance of probabilities. The respondent's goal is to show why the plaintiff's claim must fail. The respondent usually does this by putting forward their own version of the facts and/or interpretation of the law.

Although your goals are different, whether you are the plaintiff or the respondent, your job at the hearing will be essentially the same. It is to lead the decision-maker, in a series of simple, clear and convincing steps, through your version of the facts and the law, to the result that you want. You must work to make it as easy as possible for the decision-maker to accept your version of the case and decide in your favour.

Remember, success in litigation depends on three things:
1   the strength of your evidence to establish the facts;
2   whether the law applies in your favour; and
3   how well you present your case.

These are the building blocks: the facts, the law and the presentation. Presenting your case is discussed in chapter 12.

The facts

Disputes are often about the facts. The disagreement might be about what you said or promised to do, whether you did it, how you did it, why you didn't do it, whether you delivered the goods, whether they were faulty, whether you were given a chance to rectify the problem. It might be about what care arrangements you can provide for your child, whether you were properly notified about a problem, whether you can afford certain payments, what your income is, how sick you are, whether it affects your work. These types of issues are all issues of fact.

Disputes about the facts are decided on the evidence presented by both parties. Most cases are easily won or lost on the strength of a party's evidence. So it is essential that you use reliable evidence to support the facts that you assert or any fact that may be disputed.

{*Golden Rule of Litigation:* CONFIRM THE FACTS WITH EVIDENCE}

Evidence comes in many forms: verbal, written, even pictorial. Just about anything you can think of that can verify something can be used as evidence. For instance, hand-written agreements, formal contracts, invoices, receipts, quotes, bank statements, telephone records, government documents, expert reports, scale models, plans, letters, diary entries, photos, videos, the testimony of witnesses, can all be used as evidence.

Even notes taken at the time of an event might prove valuable as evidence later on. This is why it's important throughout the preparation of your case to keep an accurate record of all developments.

Obtaining the right evidence can be time consuming so you will need to collect your evidence as soon as possible. Also, with all evidence you wish to use, make sure you examine it very carefully. Does it say what you expect it says?

Before you go evidence-crazy, first, a word of warning: quality not quantity is what counts. Quality evidence ties in with exactly what you are asserting and directly verifies one or more elements of your case.

If it is indirect, vague, ambiguous or spurious, reject it and try if possible for better evidence. Sometimes though, evidence that merely favours rather than confirms your version of the facts may be the best you can get. Although this isn't ideal, it might be more than your opponent has.

If you need to provide the court or tribunal and the other party with your evidence before the hearing or as part of the claim or defence, unless otherwise requested, be sure to provide only copies and keep the originals to show at the hearing.

What follows are some simple tips on collecting the evidence you will need.

Photos, videos, digital images

These can provide excellent evidence to support your case. Not only do they add realistic and graphic detail, but by giving an accurate record of the facts, they're a form of evidence that is difficult to rebut. They provide written documentary evidence and so strengthen the probability of your case.

If you intend to use them, it's important that they're taken at the relevant time. Before and after shots are ideal. Also, the images will need to be clear and taken from an adequate distance to capture the surroundings so they give context to the shot. Take close-ups as well, to add detail to the other shots. Use a familiar item to give an idea of scale. For example, place your finger beside the scratch that has damaged the car door.

Be selective with the final choice of images. Also, be sure to record on the back of each photo or on the video or CD of photos, the details of who took the photo or video, exactly when it was taken and exactly what the images are of. Number each image you intend to use. Some cameras automatically insert the date.

Witnesses

If there is a witness to support your case, confirm with them whether they are willing to give evidence at the hearing. Although a witness is often happy to oblige without payment, they may be entitled to payment from you for their time spent at the hearing and their transport costs to and from it. Check with the registry staff of the court or tribunal whether witness expenses are applicable and what the current rate of payment is.

If there is an unwilling witness that you are certain can support your case, you may wish to **summons** or **subpoena** them. This forces them to attend the hearing and be available to give evidence and be cross-examined. To summons or subpoena a witness, you will need to draft the actual summons or subpoena according to the format of the particular court or tribunal, have it served on the witness and have a copy filed with the court or tribunal. The witness expenses would also need to be paid.

At the hearing the witness can give evidence either in person or by telephone or video link-up. If by telephone or video, give the registry staff plenty of notice so they can make the necessary arrangements.

In preparation for the hearing you might have to provide the court or tribunal and the other party with a written statement by the witness setting out their evidence. Depending on the type of case and the particular court or tribunal, it might be required in the form of an affidavit or else a signed statement. You'll find an explanation of these later in this chapter in the section 'Legal documents'.

Experts

Expert reports can be extremely valuable evidence. A report from your doctor, specialist, an engineer, architect, counsellor, consultant or health inspector can often verify particular facts of your case that are within their area of expertise and, most importantly, give an opinion about these facts. Often an expert's evidence is their opinion of what the facts are.

Where there are conflicting expert opinions offered as evidence, the decision-maker must choose between them. So a report that's clear, straightforward, authoritative and definite on the issues will have a better chance than one that is vague and non-committal.

The more authoritative the expert, the more valuable their evidence can be. For example, a report from a rheumatologist who specialises in your particular medical condition may be worth more than a report from your GP.

On the other hand, the stronger the expert's connection with your case the more important their evidence can also be. For example, a report from your family doctor of 15 years may be worth more than that of a specialist you have seen only once. The family doctor's report that documents the history of your condition, its effects on your daily life, the treatments that have been tried and how the condition has deteriorated over time can be extremely valuable as evidence. For this reason you may wish to get a report from both your specialist and your GP.

Before requesting your expert's report, think first about exactly what issue or issues the report must address and what facts it must verify. Then make the request for the report in writing. In it, explain the purpose of the report and list the specific items that need to be addressed in the report. In listing the items you want addressed, on no account tell the expert what to write in the report.

The report should contain the expert's credentials; that is, their formal qualifications and relevant experience. It should also contain the history of your contact with them and their connection with the matter in dispute as well as any facts they can verify and then their opinion on specific issues, based on your very specific questions posed in your written request.

One unfortunate reality is that what an expert says to you in conversation is sometimes quite different to what they're prepared to write down and offer as evidence. Understandably, after consideration, they may be more cautious in giving their written professional opinion.

Another unfortunate reality is that expert reports are often quite expensive. Your doctor, counsellor or other professional who sees you often might provide one free of charge, but don't expect it. It can be a time-consuming task.

When you write requesting the report, ask if they could notify you of the cost before it is prepared, so you have the opportunity to arrange for its payment or reconsider or withdraw the request. If you're on a low income you might want to also ask that there be no charge for the report, as it would cause you hardship.

The expert who provides the report may also be required as a witness at the hearing, so that their evidence can be cross-examined by the other party. Although they may be able to give their evidence by telephone or video link-up, they may still need to be paid witness expenses. This would be in addition to the cost of the expert's report. The expert witness may in the course of giving their evidence in court, need to verify that they have read the expert witness Code of Conduct.

Expert witnesses can prove quite expensive, and in some lucrative and contentious areas of law they are an industry in themselves. Make sure you clarify what costs will be involved before engaging an expert.

Government documents

Government records often contain valuable information. Your Medicare, Centrelink, Veterans' Affairs or government housing file, your medical records from a public hospital, police reports, information about development applications, planning proposals and community consultations are all examples of government documents.

If you are appealing a government decision and you need more information, or you know that a government department has a document that you need in order to prove your case, you can obtain a copy of that document or your complete file from that department. You do this using the various state or territory or federal **FOI laws.**

FOI means Freedom of Information. According to these laws, a government department must, upon request, provide you with a copy of the documents you ask for, within a specified time, unless they come within certain exceptions.

Your request may be refused, for instance, if it relates to the personal affairs of someone else or would be a breach of confidence, or would affect the national economy or security or interfere with the operations of that department. It may be refused if the document contains confidential information that could jeopardise commercial interests between the government and another party. Or it may be refused if it would take an inordinate amount of time to locate the particular document. Or else your request may be approved partially, with the release of some documents and not others, or with portions of the text blocked out.

Unfortunately, increased privatisation of government work means that more and more documents are no longer obtainable under FOI because, technically, they aren't government documents. Some arrangements have been made to overcome this, but only in limited areas.

Where FOI is available, you may be charged a fee for your FOI request, calculated on the amount of time it takes to prepare the release of the documents. Some routine requests have a fixed cost. Waiver (exemption from the fee) may be available if either the documents relate to your personal affairs or if you are on a low income and the cost would cause hardship. It is likely that the information you're requesting does relate to your personal affairs. If this is the case, in your FOI request be sure to ask for waiver of the fee and give the reason.

The trick with FOI, to have your request approved and processed smoothly and quickly, is to make the request both as specific and narrow as possible but as broad and general as necessary. This means you have to know exactly what documents to ask for. For example, within one department there may be several files in your name. There may be a payment file, a debt file, an application file and a citizen file. The information might also be on files that don't bear your name, like a property file that bears the address of the property.

Remember, too, that less and less of the crucial documents are being held in actual paper files. You might need to request, in addition to your file, all relevant computer records, including what are called screen dumps.

Before lodging your request, contact the FOI officer within the relevant department to discuss where the information you want might be located, whether it is available under FOI and how best to frame your request. Ask too about the cost and waiver requirements.

Then make your request in writing, marked to the attention of the FOI officer within that department. Some departments have their own FOI request forms. The request can generally take up to a month to process.

If the response to your FOI request is unsatisfactory, you can appeal it. The response letter you receive from the FOI officer should contain the details of how to appeal the FOI decision.

Non-government information

Information held by private companies may be available to you under provisions of the various *Privacy Acts.* For example, access to information that companies have about you, like credit records or your details held on databases, is usually granted upon request and payment of a standard fee. Contact the privacy officer of the company involved.

Medical records

You can apply for your records and medical file from a public hospital under FOI (see the previous section on 'Government documents'), by applying to the hospital's medical records department. There will be a standard fee, but ask that it be waived because it refers to your personal affairs.

You have no legal right to your medical records from a private hospital or doctor. The records belong to them. Of course, you can still request access to them, and access might be granted upon payment of a fee. But if refused, only a court order could force access to them. You could apply to the court to order that the documents be produced under subpoena, but recent cases show it is unlikely you'd succeed.

Police reports

You can generally obtain a copy of the report of police attendance at an incident involving you by applying in writing to the Police Department. There may be a fee for this report. Or, you could try formally applying for it under FOI (see the section in this chapter on 'Government documents') and asking for waiver of the fee because it concerns your personal affairs.

Other ways to obtain information

Information can also be obtained by subpoena. Check with the registry staff whether the court or tribunal you are using has subpoena powers. If so, you can issue a subpoena to produce documents, addressed to the person or business that holds the documents. This forces that person or business, within a specified time, to deliver the documents to the court where they are held for the duration of the litigation.

The return date specified on the subpoena is the date by which the documents must be delivered to the court. On that date, at a certain time, both parties can attend the court to inspect and take copies of the documents. There may be a charge, usually the reasonable expense of making the documents available.

The court or tribunal will probably have its own **subpoena** forms and procedure that you must follow. On the form, be sure to accurately identify the documents you wish to see and be sure to direct the subpoena to the right person. Within large corporations, like banks, this is often the 'public officer'.

For access to information held by the other party intended for use at the hearing, procedures of **discovery** are often available. Discovery enables you to obtain a list of documents and also to inspect the documents that the other party will be relying on. It will also give you a useful picture of the substance of their case and reduces the risk of surprises at the hearing.

Discovery also allows you to issue a set of written questions about the case that the other party must answer as part of the preparation stage of the case. These are called **interrogatories** and aim to get the other party to make certain admissions.

Discovery is quite a formal procedure. It isn't always available and might not be necessary or appropriate because the other party may be quite open about any information they have and the evidence they are using. If you decide that discovery is needed, check with the registry staff to see if it's available and what the procedures are.

If you're thinking of using the court's formal powers of subpoena, discovery or interrogatories to obtain information, get some legal advice first about whether this is necessary and whether it's the best option for getting what you need. These procedures will add to the time and expense of the case and of your opponent's case. Should you lose, these costs may be recovered from you.

Rules of evidence

To ensure a high standard of justice and at the same time protect people's rights, our legal system has developed certain rules about evidence. Under these rules, some types of evidence are not **admissible** in a court of law.

The **rules of evidence** can be found in the state and federal *Evidence Acts.* Put simply, although there are

exceptions, the basic rules of evidence are as follows:
- evidence that is irrelevant is inadmissible;
- hearsay evidence (that is, evidence that relies on what someone else alleges) is not admissible;
- opinion evidence is not admissible unless it is from an expert and is an opinion within their field of expertise;
- evidence about someone's bad character is usually inadmissible;
- evidence that is privileged information is inadmissible; evidence that would be against public policy to divulge, for example, information that threatens national security, is not admissible.

The formal rules of evidence and their application have become quite technical and are often not strictly enforced in the lower courts. Also, some specialty courts and tribunals are not bound by the rules of evidence at all or they can be dispensed with by the consent of both parties. This aims to reduce the formality and prevent complex legal arguments about the admissibility of the evidence.

In these courts and tribunals, however, this does not mean that 'anything goes'. A party can still object to a piece of evidence being accepted. The decision-maker, in deciding whether to admit the evidence, will apply common sense and may use the rules of evidence as a guide.

In relation to evidence generally, it can also be reasonably expected that the decision-maker will enforce a party's right to have adequate opportunity to examine the other party's evidence and to have adequate opportunity to respond to it.

The law

Knowing the law is as important to your case as knowing the facts. It isn't good enough to organise your evidence but neglect the legal aspect of your preparation and just rely on general principles of fairness and justice and hope that these will prevail. The legal system deals in fairness and justice every day by applying the law. So while you're obtaining and documenting your evidence, begin at once researching the relevant law.

To succeed, the law must work in your favour. You will need to be able to show how your case fulfils the necessary legal requirements and/or how the other party's does not.

This doesn't mean that when you represent yourself you are expected to become an overnight legal expert. However, you should know the law that will be applied in your case and how it will be applied to the facts.

For example, in family law, if you are trying to increase the contact hours you have with your child, the relevant legislation may say that, in determining the care arrangements for a child, the child's interests are paramount. The decision-maker, in applying the law, will look at the facts presented by both parties about the care arrangements and will weigh up which arrangements best fulfil the law; that is, which ones will be in the best interests of your child.

Now look at your facts. For instance, you may be able to show in your evidence the beneficial things you've been doing during the current contact hours and how your child might benefit from increased contact. Perhaps you have been providing after-school learning opportunities or important contact with extended family members, educational outings, or sharing time with the child's friends. Perhaps you can show valuable reasons to increase contact that are in the best interests of your child.

By researching the law and then understanding how it fits to your facts, you're developing an indispensable legal skill. This step is crucial to the preparation of your case.

{***Golden Rule of Litigation:*** KNOW THE LAW}

{***Golden Rule of Litigation:*** KNOW HOW THE LAW APPLIES TO THE FACTS}

But knowing the law isn't just about doing the research. You will also need to learn about some of the basic legal processes that courts and tribunals use. What follows are some hints on doing your legal research as well as explanations of various legal documents, information about drafting, filing, serving and **tendering documents** and a few words about the use of legal jargon.

Legal research

Often the clues to get you started on your legal research are contained in the documents you already have. For example, government decisions usually quote which law has been applied, contracts sometimes mention the laws governing that contract and, if you are the respondent, the claim itself may refer to the law relied on.

If your case involves a specific agreement, whether written or oral, the terms and conditions of that agreement will form part of the legal requirements and may well require research. Make sure you are on the right track by consulting a free legal advice service about the appropriate law for your case. Check with them what it means, how it applies and what other law or laws might benefit your case. Also check whether there are any useful cases on the subject. Keep a list of the relevant laws and cases for your quick reference.

For information about the range of free legal services available, refer back to chapter 6 'Where to go for help'. For a copy of the relevant laws, try the internet, law libraries, the largest of the public libraries or the appropriate government department. Also, for a copy of laws and cases, go to <www.austlii.edu.au>.

Other useful materials are law dictionaries, digests, casebooks, law reports, journals, case citators and regular law textbooks on the subject. There are also excellent handbooks and loose-leaf services that explain the legal requirements and procedures in specific areas of law. Always check that the information in these written resources is still current.

To understand how a particular court or tribunal is interpreting and applying a particular law or legal term, look at the relevant case law of that court or tribunal. For example, you might want to know how your Tenancy Tribunal has defined the term 'fair wear and tear' or how the Family Court is interpreting 'live separately under the one roof'. To find the relevant cases, the website of the particular court or tribunal should contain a record of its recent decisions, if not all its decisions. Also use the AUSTLII database <www.austlii.edu.au>. Search the cases selecting the particular court or tribunal.

You may wish to extend your search to the case law of other courts or tribunals. Using <www.austlii.edu.au>, search for the particular law or legal term selecting all cases.

If you do extend your search to other courts and tribunals be aware that the decision of one legal body isn't necessarily binding on another and, depending on a number of factors, it may be of little value. If you find such a case, get legal advice about its usefulness for your case.

Also be aware that sometimes the same term might have different meanings under different laws and the different meaning might not have relevance to your case. The meaning of 'income' under a *Taxation Act,* for instance, might be different to its meaning under a *Social Security Act.*

Check the definition section of the legislation involved.

If you find a case that's helpful to you, you might want to use it at the hearing as a precedent, to guide the decision-maker. If so, make sure that its facts and relevant issues apply to the circumstances of your case, and also that the case would be binding on your court or tribunal. There's nothing to be gained from confusing or misleading the decision-maker or wasting their time, using cases that are of no application to yours. Take a copy of the case and, if possible, its case citation and get legal advice about its usefulness to your case.

Case citation is a system of identifying a case according to its location in a particular law journal or law report. For centuries, important cases have been reported in various journals and reports and these have become the official record for case law. Although the internet is fast replacing the need for these journals and reports, the case citation is still the major identifier for a case.

For example in *Smith v Jones* 109 ALJR 32, *Smith v Jones* refers to the name of the case. *ALJR* means *Australian Law Journal Reports.* The number before this is the volume number and the number after is the page number. So, the case of Smith and Jones is in volume 109 of the *Australian Law Journal Reports* at page 32. Similarly, *42 NSWLR 3* means volume 42 of *New South Wales Law Reports* at page 3, and so on. Some journals and reports are issued yearly, so they are identified not by a volume number but by a year.

And when you refer to a case, for example, *Smith v Jones,* say 'Smith and Jones', not 'Smith versus Jones'. Similarly, when you refer to an Act, use its full title including its year, for example, *Disability Discrimination Act 1992.*

Apart from the laws relating to your dispute, there are also laws governing the particular court or tribunal that you are using. These Acts often have accompanying Regulations and also Rules that deal with the detail of what the court or tribunal can do and how it does it. The *Family Law Act 1975* and its accompanying *Family Law Rules,* for instance, govern the Family Court. The Victorian Supreme Court has a *Supreme Court Act 1986* and various *Supreme Court Rules* as well as a range of *Supreme Court Regulations,* which set out the powers and procedures of that court. There may also be uniform court rules, as in New South Wales under its *Civil Procedure Act 2005.*

Important information is contained in laws like these. For example, how many days you've got to lodge an appeal, the money limit on matters the court can deal with, who can make a claim, and what kinds of orders can be made.

Many courts and tribunals also issue their own Practice Directions that further refine their procedures. So, if you have a specific query about the powers or procedures of a particular court or tribunal, and the information you have received from the website, facts sheets or the registry staff doesn't satisfy you, check with these original sources.

As well, there are *Acts Interpretation Acts* in each state and territory and also federally. These laws give meanings for terms that are commonly used in legislation.

Bear in mind, there's a law for almost everything and it's easy to get sidetracked. So once you know you are on the right track, make sure you stay on it. Don't get bogged down by irrelevancies or by trying to trace everything back to its legal source. Constantly monitor the usefulness of your research and how it relates to your case.

If you're lucky, the relevant law that you're researching will be quite straightforward and commonsense. It will set out simply and clearly what must be fulfilled for the claimed remedy to be granted. If you're not so lucky, the relevant law will either be very brief with a huge body of associated case law that interprets it, or else so detailed and technical that you might as well read it backwards to understand it.

In any case, read it carefully, take a copy of the relevant excerpts, and get more legal advice if you need to. If you do get advice, take note of any key words used during the advice session for use later if you wish to consult legal textbooks or other materials.

But do not go overboard with your legal research. It will cause unnecessary panic.

At this stage of the preparation of your case, do not despair that you aren't a lawyer and don't know all the answers. If you are having problems, the best course is to admit your difficulties and get some help.

Don't despair either, if your legal research doesn't provide you with a watertight case that can be expressed in 'black-and-white' terms. Very few can. Chances are, if your case was an easy, right/wrong type it would have been resolved long ago and you wouldn't be needing to go to court now.

Equally, be cautious if you find yourself thinking you're onto a sure-fire winner. You may be missing something important. Every lawyer has a story of their latest open-and-shut case that they just lost, so be careful.

Return instead to the basics; that is, the claim, the defence and your lists. Now, using these with your legal research and by applying the law to the facts, give yourself a simple account of your case. Assess its merits.

Although you may not have a clear-cut winner, you do need to have at least an arguable case. If your best instincts, your legal research and your legal advice indicate that your chance of success is slim, you have several options. You can carry on regardless, withdraw or discontinue the case, get more advice, get a lawyer, or approach the other party and attempt a settlement. If you have any doubts about these options get more legal advice, then reassess. Be aware that if you do have no chance of success and you carry on regardless, you will not only be wasting the court's time, the other party's time and your own, but you also risk costs being awarded against you.

Legal documents

You are already familiar with legal documents like the claim and defence, but in the course of your litigation you may need to know about and provide others. Some courts and tribunals can be flexible about particular documents and can dispense with some of the requirements if you are representing yourself. Check with the registry or the website of the court or tribunal.

Here is an explanation of a few different types of legal documents. You may not need to use any of them. If you do, check with the website or registry of the court or tribunal for their specific requirements and, if possible, a sample document to help you draft your own.

An **affidavit** is a written statement accepted by the court or tribunal as evidence because its contents have been sworn or affirmed in the presence of an authorised person. It has a specific format and there are penalties for making false statements in an affidavit.

A **witness statement** is a witness's written statement that may be required by a tribunal instead of the more formal affidavit. It usually follows a simple format and is just signed and dated, not sworn or affirmed.

Both kinds of documents are written in the first person ('I') and must include the person's name, address, occupation and their version of the relevant facts; that is, the things they are verifying. In these documents, be specific about when, where and what.

A **statutory declaration** is a written statement declared before an authorised person, often a Justice of the Peace. It is similar in some ways to an affidavit but does not carry as much weight in a court or tribunal.

A **certified copy** of a document verifies that it is a true copy of the document. On the copy are the words or a stamp that says 'this is a true copy of such-and-such document'. It is then signed and dated, usually by a certified person, like a Justice of the Peace (JP) or solicitor.

A **statement of issues** and a **statement of facts and contentions** are documents required by some tribunals. Both parties generally need to provide them, but there may be exemptions if you are self-represented. These statements give the decision-maker a useful picture of the dispute from both sides. As it says, the first one is to clarify the issues, so it will probably be short. The second one, however, tells the story of the case (the facts) and then how those facts satisfy the law (the contentions), so it will be longer. With both types of statement, remember to sign and date the document.

A **certificate of readiness** signals that the preparations are completed and the case is ready for hearing. In it you estimate the length of time needed for the hearing, how many witnesses you will be calling and, if any, the details of the lawyer representing you. It might have a different name, like **compliance certificate** or **hearing information form.**

A **notice of discontinuance** is lodged by the plaintiff. It notifies the court or tribunal that you are withdrawing the claim. It may have another name, like **notice of withdrawal.**

A **notice of motion** is a way of petitioning the court, especially a higher court like the Supreme Court. In it, you formally apply to the court to make certain orders. Many legal actions are started with a notice of motion.

General rules for drafting legal documents

The degree of formality required for drafting documents varies with the type of case and the court or tribunal involved. Again, you may be able to get a sample of the particular document from the website or registry.

Although each court and tribunal has its own requirements of style and format, there are also some general rules for drafting any legal document so that the other party and the court or tribunal can identify its basics at a glance.

The document will begin with the full title of the court or tribunal, the matter or file number of the case and the names of the parties, with their title, such as plaintiff and respondent. Then comes the title of the actual document and its substance.

Often each paragraph of the substance of the document is numbered and generally concludes with the signature and title of the person or their lawyer. At the bottom of the first page, at least, is a line, then a footer, giving the name and address of the source of the document. It might be the name and address of the lawyer who prepared the document and it is the address for service of documents on that party. If you are representing yourself, put your own name and address for service of documents on you.

Filing and serving documents

To file a document you lodge it at the registry of the court or tribunal and, if required, pay a filing fee. Once it is accepted and stamped, it is considered filed. Usually extra photocopies of the document need to be filed together with the original.

The courts are developing some capacity for filing documents online. While still limited in its scope and application, this procedure will eventually become more widely available.

Service of a document is its delivery to the other party or their lawyer. There are rules and time limits for serving a document. Check whether it can be served by post or fax, or whether it must be served in person.

If it needs to be served in person, it must be hand delivered. You can do this yourself or arrange for a process server to do it. For service in person, an **affidavit of service** may need to be completed by the person who served it. This verifies the delivery. Check with the registry or website.

Be sure to obey any time limits for lodging documents. If this time limit expires, you may need to apply for an **extension of time** or get **leave to apply out of time.** This means getting special permission from the court or tribunal and there's no guarantee you'll get it.

{*Golden Rule of Litigation:* OBEY THE TIME LIMITS FOR LODGING DOCUMENTS}

Tendering documents

Documents are tendered by presenting them to the court in the course of the hearing. Generally it is important to tender the originals of the documents, not copies. Copies can be used but are generally not considered to be the best evidence.

You can tender documents at the beginning of your presentation or throughout. It is a good idea to have an extra copy of the document to give the other party for their records. The other party can object to the tendering of a document in the same way as with other evidence, for example, if it is irrelevant or it contains hearsay. If you wish to question a witness about information contained in a certain document, you may need to tender the document and have it accepted by the court before asking the questions.

Documents that are tendered remain with the court until after the hearing is finalised. They are often returned to you by mail some time after the result.

Legal jargon

Congratulations! You have already digested an enormous stock of legal jargon. You're now familiar with terms like plaintiff, respondent, claim, defence, cross-claim, counter claim, default judgment, limitation date, extension of time, without prejudice, summons, subpoena, waiver, affidavit, service and tendering. These are some of the basics in the jargon of litigation.

A well-known trick of lawyers opposing you when you represent yourself is to try to confuse and intimidate you with lots of unnecessary jargon. This ploy can be easily short-circuited if each time you hear a term you don't understand, you ask its meaning.

Whenever and wherever you come across jargon that is relevant to your case, whether it's in a phone call, a letter or court document or said by a lawyer, a court official or judge, ask for an explanation. If the explanation is full of jargon, respectfully ask again. Ask someone else. Do more research. Get some legal advice. Keep asking until you are satisfied. Of course, avoid being belligerent or aggressive, as it will only alienate the party or the court, but make sure you find out.

If you're afraid to ask questions, you risk losing control of your case unnecessarily. It will be of no use to you if you find out too late what a crucial term meant or what the main argument was about. It will be of no use either if you are intimidated into paralysis by an opponent whose only advantage is an oversupply of jargon.

Our legal system tries hard to be accessible to everyone, not just lawyers. And unlike a lawyer, you have no precious credentials to protect. So go ahead and ask, ask, ask all those silly sounding, honest questions and don't be embarrassed in the least. You'll be surprised what you can learn from them and the confidence you'll gain too, from knowing exactly what's going on.

{**Golden Rule of Litigation:** DON'T BE AFRAID TO ASK QUESTIONS}

12

Preparing your case part 3

The presentation at the hearing is the final building block in the preparation of your case, and luckily, much of the groundwork is already completed. By now you have compiled your lists, collected your evidence and researched the law. You are familiar with your own and your opponent's case as well as with the litigation process itself. How successfully you present your case in court will depend on your ability to know and use this groundwork thoroughly.

The steps to prepare the presentation for the hearing are similar for both the plaintiff and the respondent, although the orientation will be different because the goals are different. If you are the plaintiff, remember the burden is on you to adequately prove the claim you're making and you must prove it on the balance of probabilities. If you are the respondent, you must show how and why the plaintiff's claim must fail.

There are three stages to the formation of your presentation for the hearing. The first is to revisit all the details of your case and to organise them into a preliminary outline. This will provide a rough sketch of the elements necessary to establish your case. It will bring together the law and evidence and will order your evidence into its natural sequence. The next stage is to reshape this preliminary outline into a main outline that fits the framework of the hearing. The third step is to summarise your main outline in point form to use as a prompt to guide you through your presentation at the hearing.

Allow yourself enough time before the hearing date to prepare your case properly. You'll need time to structure your presentation, organise your paperwork, check details and make final preparations. But just as important, also give yourself time to think through the facts and issues carefully and convert your thoughts to clear argument.

Doing this will yield a number of benefits. It will finalise your approach to the case and consolidate all you have learnt so far. It will improve the quality of your preparation and help you construct a more coherent, persuasive presentation. And it will restore calm if you have any fuzzy confusion or mounting panic. This thorough preparation will be your best antidote to nerves at the hearing.

And by all means, while you are making your final preparations, keep alive any negotiations to settle the case. Most settlements occur just before the hearing.

Stage 1. The preliminary outline

Much of the work for your preliminary outline has already been done in the lists you compiled for the preparation of your claim or defence. Using your chronology and your lists, prepare your outline following the guidelines on the next page.

When you have completed your preliminary outline, examine it closely and take the time to consider your case as whole. Review again, what is its essence? What are the issues? Are they factual? Legal? Are they a combination? Consider the other party's case. Are their claims wrong? How? Have they missed something crucial? Have you? Now make any necessary changes to your outline.

What follows below are four simple examples of the way you might approach preparing a preliminary outline. One involves a plaintiff in a tenancy matter, the second is a plaintiff's case in a consumer matter, the third is a respondent's in a family law dispute, and the fourth concerns an applicant's appeal of a government decision.

The purpose of the examples is to show you how to structure a preliminary outline. For their maximum application and because laws vary so much from state to state and change so often, all the laws and cases mentioned are completely fictional and will not accurately reflect the law. Do not rely on them in the preparation of your own case.

PRELIMINARY OUTLINE

1 WHAT I WANT Begin by reviewing and itemising exactly what remedies you want from the case. If you are the plaintiff, consult your claim. If you're the respondent, consult the claim and your defence.

2 FACTS AND EVIDENCE Next, using your chronology and other lists, compile a concise account of the necessary facts in point form. Alongside a fact, itemise in brackets what evidence you will use to confirm the fact.

3 LAW Next, set out the relevant provisions of the law that apply to your dispute. If your dispute involves an agreement, include the relevant clauses of that agreement. Also specify any relevant cases. In brackets, note down that you will need to provide a copy of the case at the hearing.

4 THE OTHER PARTY'S CASE Where you are aware of the substance of the other party's case, outline it.

5 ARGUMENT Next, formulate the argument section of your outline by applying the law to your facts,

showing how the law applies in your favour. Include in this section, the reasons why the other party's case should fail. For example, point out how the evidence or law doesn't support their case or how their evidence isn't adequate to prove their case or how yours is better than theirs. This argument section of your outline explains why you should get what you want.

    6 SUMMARY Give a brief summary of the case in three or four sentences.

    7 CASE IN A NUTSHELL Finally, express exactly what your case is, in a nutshell. Explain it in one or two sentences.

PRELIMINARY OUTLINE
Example 1

Plaintiff's case in a tenancy dispute
ALL LAWS AND CASES USED IN THIS EXAMPLE ARE FICTITIOUS.
DO NOT USE THEM IN THE PREPARATION OF YOUR CASE.

    You are the plaintiff and landlord of a property. Your last tenants left the premises in less than ideal condition and refuse to rectify the situation. You have lodged a bond dispute claim because you would like the cost of repairs to come out of the tenants' bond. You might prepare an outline like this.

1 What I want

An order that $1180 be paid to me by the tenants from the rental bond as compensation for the damage to my rental premises.

Being for:

Carpet cleaning & replacement	$640
Bathroom basin replacement	$240
Replacement of destroyed curtains	$260
Plus	
Claim filing fee	$40
TOTAL	$1,180

2 Facts and evidence

Tenancy Agreement entered 3 August 2007.

(COPY OF TENANCY AGREEMENT 3/8/07)

(BOND LODGEMENT RECEIPT 7/8/07)

(COPY OF CONDITION REPORT 3/8/07)

Tenancy Agreement shows:

Tenants: John and Sue Smith.

Property: 3 Gould Lane, Bensfield. Term: 12 months. Rent: $340 per week. Bond: $1200.

Condition Report shows: condition of carpet 'excellent', condition of all curtains 'fair', condition of bathroom 'clean and tidy'. There is no mention in the condition report of any chip or crack or problem with the bathroom basin. Tenancy ended 3 August 2008.

Final Inspection of premises carried out 3/8/08. (COPY OF FINAL INSPECTION REPORT 3/8/08)

Final Inspection Report shows: carpet in three of the rooms is 'stained', bathroom basin 'chipped and cracked', curtains 'torn'.

Photos taken 3/8/08 show details of damage. (6 PHOTOS OF DAMAGE 3/8/08)

Age of carpet at end of tenancy: 3 years.

(RECEIPT FOR LAYING OF NEW CARPET DATED 12/12/05)

Age of premises and all fittings at end of the tenancy: 10 years.

3/8/08 Repairs requested verbally, request refused, damage disputed as 'fair wear and tear'.

4/8/08 Bond dispute form and claim lodged.

5/8/08 Carpet cleaned, cleaning unsatisfactory, replacement recommended. (QUOTE, RECEIPT AND LETTER OF RECOMMENDED ACTION FROM NIFTY CARPET CLEANING CO.)

5/8/08 Quotes obtained for new basin and curtains, similar in standard to those damaged.

(QUOTES FROM BATHROOMS GALORE, SUPERIOR BASINS, READYMADE CURTAINS)

The premises are not covered by insurance for this damage.

3 Law

Section 65 of the *Tenancy Act 1989* gives the Tribunal power to make the order I want. It states: 'The Tribunal may, in any proceedings before it, make any one or more of the following orders:

(a) an order for which an application may be made by any person under this Act;

(b) an order arising out of the Tribunal's jurisdiction with respect to rental bonds.'

Clause 20 of the Tenancy Agreement makes the tenant liable for damage that is not fair wear and tear. It states: 'The tenant agrees: when the agreement ends, to leave the premises as nearly as possible in the same condition (fair wear and tear excepted) as set out in the condition report for these residential premises.'

Section 15 of the *Tenancy Act 1989* states: 'The parties are required to minimise their loss from breach of the Tenancy Agreement.'

Relevant cases on fair wear and tear:

Mills v Boon (2004): Fair wear and tear is the damage reasonably expected to happen in the 'normal helter skelter of daily life'. (COPY OF *MILLS V BOON* CASE)

Smith v Jones (2003): The length of the tenancy and the age of the carpet are factors to be considered in relation to damage, fair wear and tear and compensation. (COPY OF *SMITH V JONES* CASE)

4 The respondents' case

The respondents deny the extent of the damage and assert that the damage is fair wear and tear. Their evidence will be oral. Any other evidence is unknown.

5 Argument

The tenants have breached clause 20 of the Tenancy

Agreement and are liable for the damage to the premises. The photos and final inspection report clearly show that when the tenancy ended, the tenants did not leave the premises, as nearly as possible, in the same condition as set out in the condition report.

The extent of the damage, as shown by the photos, is not fair wear and tear as it is in excess of 'the normal helter skelter of daily life'. Damage due to normal helter skelter of daily life would not warrant the replacement of carpet within its first three years and replacement of the bathroom basin and curtains within ten years.

I have complied with the requirement of section 15 of the *Tenancy Act 1989* to minimise my loss by obtaining a number of quotes before having the repairs carried out and choosing the cheapest of them. As the items were relatively new and were not due for replacement, I claim the full cost of replacement.

6 Summary

Bond dispute: Claim for $1180.

Damage to property during tenancy: carpet basin curtains

Not fair wear and tear:

Evidence: condition report

final inspection report

photos

quotes

letter recommending replacement of carpet receipts

Law: Under tenancy agreement, tenants are liable for damage except for fair wear and tear. Evidence and cases support that the damage here was not fair wear and tear. I have minimised my loss.

7 Case in a nutshell The damage done to the premises during the tenancy is not fair wear and tear. The tenants are liable.

PRELIMINARY OUTLINE

Example 2

Plaintiff's case in a consumer matter

ALL LAWS AND CASES USED IN THIS EXAMPLE ARE FICTITIOUS.

DO NOT USE THEM IN THE PREPARATION OF YOUR CASE.

You are the owner of a home that was built three years ago. The roof leaks and despite numerous requests, the builder has not returned to fix it.

1 What I want

An order that the respondent pay me $7725 for the repair of the roof of my home plus $40 for the cost of the filing fee plus interest pursuant to the *Small Claims Act 1993* calculated at 9 per cent per annum from the date of the damage occurring.

2 Facts and evidence

June–December 2005 home built by Easy Build Ltd, Builders Licence No 344402.

(BUILDING CERTIFICATE DATED DECEMBER 2005)

December 2006 Home purchased by me. (COPY OF CERTIFICATE OF TITLE)

January 2008 Roof began leaking.

January 2008 Letters sent to builder requesting repairs under

Builder's Warranty. (COPY OF TWO LETTERS SENT DATED 4/1/08 AND 28/1/08)

February 2008 Inspection by Office of Fair Trading,

Rectification Order issued to builder. (COPY OF BUILDING REPORT AND RECTIFICATION ORDER DATED 20/2/08) February–May 2008 Problem not rectified. No action taken by builder.

(PHOTOS OF CURRENT STATE OF ROOF AND RAIN DAMAGE TO CEILING, DATED 2/7/08)

15 June 2008 Two quotes obtained for repair of roof. (TWO QUOTES)

1 July 2008 Claim issued.

3 Law

Section 20(c) *House Building Act 2001* provides the following warranty for the building of new dwellings: 'a warranty that, if the work consists of the construction of a dwelling, the work will result, to the extent of the work conducted, in a dwelling that is reasonably fit for occupation as a dwelling.'

Section 45 *House Building Act 2001* states: 'The warranty shall be for a period of seven years from the date of completion of construction.'

4 The other party's case

The respondent denies that the damage has resulted from poor construction of the roof. Respondent's evidence is a letter to me from him dated 20 July 2007 referring to his extensive experience in the building industry.

5 Argument

The warranty created by the *House Building Act 2001* applies to this home because it is less than seven years since completion of its construction. Under the warranty, the builder is liable to construct a building that's reasonably fit for occupation as a dwelling. The Building Report and the

Rectification Order carried out by the Office of Fair Trading expressly state that the poor construction of the roof has resulted in the home not being reasonably fit for occupation as a dwelling. The builder is therefore liable for repairing the roof.

6 Summary

Builder's Warranty case. The home is less than seven years old. Poor construction of the roof has resulted in damage, making the home not fit to occupy. The builder is liable. I have notified the builder of the problem and requested that he fix it. He has not fixed it.

7 Case in a nutshell

Under the House Building Warranty the builder is liable for the cost of repairing the roof of my home to make it fit for occupation.

PRELIMINARY OUTLINE

Example 3

Respondent's case in a family law matter ALL LAWS AND CASES USED IN THIS EXAMPLE ARE FICTITIOUS.

DO NOT USE THEM IN THE PREPARATON OF YOUR CASE.

You are divorced and have primary care of your three-year-old son. Your ex-husband has contact with your son according to the arrangements set out in the Final Orders granted by the Family Court. But there have been compliance problems with these arrangements. And now your ex-husband wishes to take your son to Italy for two weeks to visit extended family. He has applied to the Family Court to change the Final Orders to allow this trip. You are afraid that if he goes overseas with the child he will not return.

1 What I want

(A) The applicant's Application to Vary the Final Orders be dismissed;

(B) An order made placing the child's name on the Federal Police Airport Watch List.

2 Facts and evidence

The Final Orders, granted 4/5/07, set out the current contact arrangements for Jason aged three years. They provide for contact with the applicant father each alternate weekend from 4pm Friday to 4pm Sunday plus one week four times a year plus Christmas day. (COPY OF FINAL ORDERS) There have been a number of compliance problems with these orders. Since 4/5/07 there have only been two blocks of one-week contact with the applicant father instead of the five blocks possible under the Final Orders. Lack of contact has been due to the applicant cancelling the arranged blocks at short notice. As well there have been the following other problems:

14/6/07 Applicant late in returning Jason to my care after contact.

17/8/07 Applicant late in returning Jason to my care after weekend contact.

19/1/08 Applicant late in returning Jason to my care after weekend contact.

10/7/08 Applicant late in returning Jason to my care after weekend contact. On that day there was an argument between the applicant and myself, in front of my mother, about returning Jason late to my care. During the argument the applicant threatened to take the child and never return. (COPY OF MY AFFIDAVIT ACCOMPANYING MY RESPONSE TO THE APPLICANT'S APPLICATION DATED 9/10/08) (COPY OF AFFIDAVIT OF MY MOTHER, SUE ANN BEST, DATED 9/10/08)

(COPY OF MY EMAIL TO APPLICANT, DATED 19/7/07, COMPLAINING OF HIS CONDUCT) (COPY OF HIS REPLY, DATED 20/7/08)

6/8/08 Applicant sold his home in Australia and his car. Applicant owns a home in Italy and has family there. He holds an Australian and Italian passport.

(COPY OF AFFIDAVIT OF MUTUAL FRIEND DOROTHY ANN KELLERS DATED 2/10/08)

10/9/08 Applicant lodged Application for the Final Orders to be varied to allow the applicant to take Jason to Italy for 14 days between 2 December 2008 and 16 December

2008 to visit the child's paternal grandmother.

10/10/08 I lodged my response to the application, including affidavits.

3 Law

Under section 65Y of the *Family Law Act 1975:* 'A party cannot take the child out of Australia unless either

(a) both parties agree in writing; or

(b) the court makes an order allowing it.' Section 68F *Family Law Act 1975* sets out the matters that the court must consider when deciding what parenting and contact arrangements will promote the best interests of the child.

Subsections (c), (h), (j) and (k) are relevant here:

(c) the likely effect of any change in the child's circumstances, including the likely effect on the child of any separation from either parent;

(h) the attitude to the child and the responsibilities of parenthood as displayed by the relevant parties;

(j) those orders least likely to lead to the institution of further proceedings;

(k) any other fact or circumstance.

Cases:

X v Y (2002). In that case, the Family Court found that the father's threats to abduct the child constituted a real risk that he would remove the child from the country unlawfully and the Court granted orders that the child's name be placed on the AFP Airport Watch List.

4 The applicant's case

The applicant claims that his wish to take Jason to meet and bond with his family in Italy is in the best interests of the child and that the trip shared together is an important element of parenting.

The applicant claims the breaches of previous orders were minor aberrations and were due to misunderstandings between the parties.

The applicant claims the duration of the separation (two weeks) is not a substantial separation of the child from his mother and will not adversely affect the child.

The applicant agrees to telephone me daily from Italy so that I can speak to Jason. The applicant denies that he intends not to return to Australia with Jason.

The applicant agrees, if required by the Court, to deposit a $30 000 bond as security against Jason not returning.

The applicant also argues that Italy is a signatory to the Hague Convention and this would help secure the return of Jason if he and Jason did not return.

5 Argument

(A) That the applicant's Application to Vary the Final Orders be dismissed:

Applying the factors set out in section 68F *Family Law Act 1975*, it is not in the best interests of the child to change the contact arrangements to allow the applicant to take Jason, aged three, on a two-week overseas trip:

Subsection 68F (c): the likely effect of the two-week separation from his mother:

Jason is not accustomed to such an extended separation. He has never been away for two weeks from his mother.

Apart from alternate weekends with the applicant, the child has only had two blocks of one-week contact. At age three, Jason still requires substantial care and is accustomed to full-time care provided by the mother. Given the history of broken arrangements, it is also unlikely the applicant would honour his promise of making the telephone calls from Italy.

Subsection 68F (h): the applicant's attitude to the child and the responsibilities of parenthood:

Since the Final Orders were granted, the applicant has breached them on many occasions by returning Jason late and by cancelling three of the five one-week block visits. In addition he has made threats to abduct Jason.

To date, the applicant has not discharged his parenting responsibilities well. He has been neither conscientious nor co-operative and hasn't shown an appropriate attitude to these responsibilities nor appropriate respect for the Court's orders.

Subsection 68F (j): the risk of further proceedings if the Final Orders are changed to allow the overseas visit:

The applicant's threats to abduct Jason show that a real risk exists that, if allowed to take Jason to Italy, he may not return. The applicant has recently disposed of his property in Australia but owns property in Italy. He has no other family or strong ties in Australia apart from Jason. His family ties are in Italy. If Jason is not returned to Australia at the end of the two-week period, further applications to the Family Court will be necessary to secure his return. The services of the Italian government may also be needed. Although Australia is a signatory to the Hague Convention, this may improve the chances of the return of the child but does not guarantee it.

The deposit of a $30 000 bond may not cover the expenses of court proceedings and further action to recover the child and, given the substantial recent income earned from selling assets in Australia, may not be a sufficient deterrent to the applicant.

Subsection 68F (k): any other fact or circumstance: The threat made by the applicant to myself in the presence of my mother that the applicant would take the child one day and never return is a significant factor in considering whether to grant the variation of the Final Orders.

(B) That an order be made placing the child's name on the Federal Police Airport Watch List:

The threat to abduct Jason also shows that, should the application to Vary the Final Orders be denied, there is a real risk that the applicant may try to take Jason out of the country unlawfully. As in the case of *X v Y* (2002), where the facts were similar and the extent of the risk was similar, such an order was made. On the balance of probabilities, an order placing Jason's name on the Federal Police Airport Watch List is justified.

6 Summary

Applying the factors outlined in section 68F *Family Law Act 1975,* the applicant's application to Vary the Final Orders to allow Jason aged three years to travel to Italy with his father for 14 days should be dismissed.

Applying the case *X v Y* (2002), my application for an order placing the child's name on the AFP Airport Watch List should be granted.

7 Case in a nutshell

It is not in the best interests of the child to vary the Final Orders.

It is in the best interests of the child to have his name put on the AFP Airport Watch List and such an order is justified in the present circumstances.

PRELIMINARY OUTLINE
Example 4

Applicant's case in an appeal of a government decision

ALL LAWS AND CASES USED IN THIS EXAMPLE ARE FICTITIOUS.

DO NOT USE THEM IN THE PREPARATION OF YOUR CASE.

Due to a Centrelink computer error, you have been overpaid $3200 in Family Tax Benefit. You were mistakenly paid your entitlement twice. Now Centrelink says you should have known you weren't entitled to the double payment and you should have notified them. Centrelink wants the money back and is withholding $40 per fortnight from your Family Tax Benefit to repay the debt. You have decided to appeal the government decision that says you must repay the debt.

1 What I want

The decision of the Secretary, Department of Family and Community Services, that I owe a Family Tax Benefit debt of $3200 set aside.

2 Facts and evidence

14 February 2007 I received advice from Centrelink to overestimate my

income for purposes of receiving Family Tax Benefit to avoid risk of an overpayment. Any income shortfall would be reconciled by the Australian Tax Office (ATO) at the end of the financial year with my tax return and, if entitled, I would receive a top-up payment of Family Tax Benefit.

23 February 2007 I lodged Family Tax Benefit Application. (T DOC page 23)

March–December 2007 I received Family Tax Benefit of $110 per fortnight for my two children, Amy and Tan. (T DOC page 24)

1 September 2007 I lodged my tax return. (COPY OF TAX RETURN)

1–10 December 2007 I phoned Centrelink three times asking about top-up payment. I was advised each time that the ATO was doing the reconciliation. I requested that any top-up amount be deposited into my bank account that received the regular FTB payments. During each of these telephone calls with Centrelink I was advised to contact ATO.

(SCREEN DUMPS OF NOTES BY CENTRELINK OFFICER OF THE PHONECALLS. T DOCS pages 26, 27, 31)

1-10 December 2007 I phoned ATO twice, asking about the reconciliation. Each time I was advised to call Centrelink.

13 December 2007 I received cheque for $3200 in the mail, with no accompanying letter from either Centrelink or ATO itemising my entitlement. It was unclear whether cheque was from ATO or Centrelink.

15 December 2007 $3200 was deposited by Centrelink in my bank account. (SCREEN DUMP OF TRANSACTION. T DOC page 34)

18 December 2007 Letter received from Centrelink advising of bank deposit. (CENTRELINK LETTER DATED 15 DECEMBER. T DOC page 35)

23 January 2008 Letter from Centrelink advising of overpayment of $3200, caused by a double payment of the entitled amount. (T DOC page 37)

No actual details of the reconciliation were ever received, either from Centrelink or ATO.

My financial position is as follows:

Household income: The household consists of myself (widowed two years ago), mother-in-law, two school-aged children and two adult children. My wage of $50 000 per year is the sole income for the household plus the FTB of $110 per fortnight received for the school-aged children. I have various medical problems requiring regular, costly medication. (COPY OF LETTER FROM GP) At present Centrelink is withholding $40 of the $110 per fortnight to repay the debt.

I have received infrequent financial assistance from the Salvation Army and from my brother-in-law during 2007. (COPY OF LETTER FROM SALVATION ARMY FINANCIAL COUNSELLOR; COPY OF LETTER FROM BROTHER-IN-LAW DETAILING HIS LOANS TO ME)

Assets: Home valued at $450 000 mortgaged for $300 000. Mortgage repayments are $24 000 per year.

(COPY OF HOME LOAN BANK STATEMENT); car worth $4000 (COPY OF REGISTRATION PAPERS); furniture worth approx $3000. Expenses: As outlined in Income and Expenditure Statement, prepared with the help of the financial counsellor at the Salvation Army. (COPY OF I & E STATEMENT AND LETTER FROM FINANCIAL COUNSELLOR; COPY OF PHONE, ELECTRICITY, RATES, SCHOOL FEES AND PHARMACY BILLS; COPY OF LETTER FROM PRINCIPAL, MARIST SCHOOL, OUTLINING FEE RELIEF PROVIDED FOR THE TWO CHILDREN)

3 Law

Section 1234 *Social Insecurity Act 1998* states: 'Subject to subsection (2), the right to recover a debt, that is caused solely by administrative error made by the Commonwealth, is waived if the debtor received the payment in good faith.' Subsection 2 of section 1234 *Social Insecurity Act 1998* states: 'The financial circumstances of the debtor must be such that repayment of the debt would cause severe financial hardship to the debtor.'

Cases:

Secretary, Department of Social Security v Ted Fred (1996) 1 FLR 123: The payment can't be said to have been received in good faith if the recipient knew or had good reason to know that he or she isn't entitled to the payments received. (COPY OF TED FRED CASE)

Secretary, Department of Family and Community Services v Fooey (2003) ALD 64: payment can't be said to have been received in good faith if the recipient turned a blind eye to the circumstances that raise doubt as to the entitlement and the person refused to make reasonable inquiries where such doubt exists. (COPY OF FOOEY CASE)

Secretary, Department of Family and Community Services v Tiddles (2003) ALD 32: Severe financial hardship goes beyond mere straitened financial circumstances and includes suffering of a severe or extreme nature. (COPY OF TIDDLES CASE)

Secretary, Department of Family and Community Services v Bambam (2005) ALD 44: The family's financial circumstances are such that the family 'is going out backwards. Relief from this debt will not solve their financial problems but will release them from a further additional burden'. (COPY OF BAMBAM CASE)

4 Centrelink's case

That there is an overpayment of $3200, that it was not received in good faith, as I should have known that I was not entitled to two payments of the same amount, and that I am not suffering severe financial hardship.

5 Argument

I concede that there is a debt, caused by double payment of my entitled top-up Family Tax Benefit.

Administrative error issue: The overpayment was caused solely by administrative error by the Commonwealth. The overpayment didn't occur through any fault of mine. At all stages I fulfilled what was required of me for the FTB to be assessed and paid correctly. In fact, upon advice from Centrelink, I overestimated my income to begin with, to avoid an overpayment.

Good faith issue: I did not know that I was not entitled to a cheque from ATO and a payment from Centrelink. When I did inquire about the top-up payment, I was shuttle-cocked back and forth between Centrelink and the ATO and it was unclear who had responsibility for what. The records of my telephone calls with Centrelink do not show that Centrelink clarified where the payment would be coming from or how much it would be for. The only letter regarding any payment was not received until after both payments had been given to me and the letter was ambiguous, when read in light of the circumstances of my payment. I did not make further inquiries when I received both payments because I had no reason to doubt my entitlement.

In reference to the Ted Fred and Fooey cases, I did receive the payments in good faith, as in the circumstances I had no good reason to know that I was entitled or to doubt my entitlement to both payments.

Severe financial hardship issue: Since the death of my husband two years ago I have been going backwards at a rate of knots. I am struggling to keep the family home. I have received help from the Salvation Army and my brother-in-law, but cannot expect to continue relying on this charity indefinitely. My medical condition has stabilised so that I can continue working, but I need to continue with the medication. My two adult children have not had an income to contribute to the household for 18 months.

Since the Tiddles case of 2003, severe financial hardship has been further defined, by the Bambam case, to include circumstances similar to mine.

6 Summary

There is an overpayment of Family Tax Benefit of $3200. It is attributable solely to an administrative error made by the Commonwealth. The duplicate payments weren't made through any fault of mine. I received the payments in good faith. I reasonably thought that Centrelink and the ATO shared equal responsibility for the top-up FTB payment so I had no reason to know or doubt that I wasn't entitled to both payments. None of the evidence supports Centrelink's case that I should've known I wasn't entitled or made further inquiries to ascertain my entitlement.

My financial situation is becoming dire since my husband's death as I struggle to keep the family home, rear a family and support dependent extended family and adult children. For these reasons, under the provisions of the *Social Insecurity Act 1998*, I should not have to repay the overpayment.

7 Case in a nutshell

According to Section 1234 of the *Social Insecurity Act 1998*, the Commonwealth should not recover this debt because the overpayment is due solely to the Commonwealth's

> administrative error, I received it in good faith and recovery of the debt would cause me severe or extreme financial hardship.

Your preliminary outline sets out the logical steps needed to establish your case. It also shows, with the bracketed sections, how to order your evidence and other paperwork and where it fits as you steadily build your case.

As it is though, your preliminary outline doesn't quite fit into the format of a hearing. It still needs some fine-tuning. To transform it into a fully functional presentation for the hearing, you first need to know more about the hearing itself.

How a hearing works

The conduct of hearings varies greatly, but most follow the pattern below. Check this with your court or tribunal.

> **HOW A HEARING WORKS**
> Housekeeping matters

> then
> Plaintiff's introduction and evidence
> then
> Respondent's introduction and evidence
> then
> Plaintiff's argument and summary
> then
> Respondent's argument and summary
> then
> Plaintiff's reply (if necessary) And respondent's reply (if necessary)
> then
> Result

The hearing usually begins with any housekeeping matters that affect the progress of the hearing. These are often procedural things like last-minute changes to the availability of witnesses or amendments to documents already before the court or tribunal. When these are dealt with, the plaintiff's case begins.

The plaintiff or applicant always presents their case first. Generally, they start with a brief introduction of what the whole case is about and what their case involves, in a nutshell. Then they proceed with presenting their evidence. They tender documents, drawing attention to salient features, and present their witnesses.

The evidence of the plaintiff's witnesses is taken one at a time. The witness is called into the room, goes to the witness box, is sworn in and then questioned, first by the plaintiff.

The party providing the witness always questions their witness first and the questions must cover all of the witness's evidence. This is called **examination-in-chief.** Then the other party, here the respondent, questions the witness, called **cross-examination.**

Then the plaintiff can ask any follow-up questions arising from the cross-examination. This is called **re-examination.** After reexamination, the witness is dismissed from the witness box and the next of the plaintiff's witnesses is called.

Any documents that specifically relate to the witness's evidence may be tendered to the court during the questioning. For example, if the witness has made an affidavit, the examination-in-chief will probably begin with the tendering of this affidavit. Other relevant documents may be tendered during the questioning, with the witness being specifically asked for their response to the contents of the document.

When the plaintiff has finished presenting their evidence, it's the respondent's turn to present this first part of their case in a similar fashion. The respondent begins with a brief introduction about their case and how it differs from the plaintiff's version, what it is about, in a nutshell.

Then the respondent presents their evidence. Documents are tendered and attention is drawn to the relevant parts and the respondent's witnesses are called. One by one the witnesses are examined-in-chief by the respondent, cross-examined by the plaintiff, then if necessary, re-examined by the respondent.

Much of the hearing time can be spent dealing with the parties' evidence. It is often the most important part of each party's case. After all, the evidence establishes the story of the case.

Once the plaintiff and respondent have finished with the evidence, the plaintiff presents their arguments. This part of the presentation, called **submissions,** includes a discussion of the relevant law, a review of the evidence and an explanation of how the law applies to the facts and applies favourably to their case. It also includes any arguments against the other party's case. Written submissions may also be tendered in addition to the verbal submissions. Often the plaintiff completes their presentation with a brief summary.

After this, the respondent presents their submissions and concludes by summarising their case. If needed, the plaintiff can reply to the respondent's arguments or summary with further submissions and, if needed, the respondent can then respond also.

This usually ends the parties' involvement in the hearing. The decision-maker may then give the result immediately or might **reserve the**

decision, that is, announce it at a later date.

Many informal tribunals use a simpler format for the hearing. Their pattern can be as straightforward as having the plaintiff's (or applicant's) whole case heard first, followed by the respondent's, with the plaintiff having the right of reply at the end. The presentation generally contains the same elements in the same order (that is, housekeeping matters, introduction, evidence, submissions and summary) but it is heard in one block.

Some tribunals are simpler still. Using an inquisitorial approach, the decision-maker may entirely control the direction of the hearing. Having read the paperwork beforehand, they may begin with their own questions about the issues of the case and proceed from there. With this format, the parties still need to prepare their presentation along the same lines (that is, housekeeping, introduction, evidence, arguments, summary) but as always, at the hearing they may need to improvise.

The best way to learn how your hearing will work is to watch one in action. Most hearings are open to the public, so contact the registry about cases similar to yours or check the website for the daily listings of hearings. See for yourself how the decision-maker and staff handle the matters and how the lawyers and parties conduct themselves. Observe the format, the procedures and the degree of formality. Take notes. It will be well worth your while.

Technological advances are now allowing the legal system to dispense with expensive courtroom time by conducting some hearings via the internet. Still in the infant stages, developments at present allow lawyers on both sides, in appropriate cases, to lodge documents, submissions and evidence online and the decision-maker decides the case from this and notifies the lawyers of the result. In time, this method will be extended to a greater variety of cases and may well be available to you. If it is available, you will need to follow the process carefully and attend promptly to its requirements.

A small number of legal bodies deal with and decide a case solely on the basis of the documents provided and no actual hearing between the parties takes place. If your case is to be dealt with in this way, check your paperwork very carefully before submitting it. Be sure that it covers all the aspects of your case. In this and any other non-traditional format for a case, still prepare your outlines in the usual way. They will be of great benefit to the drafting of your submissions, the ordering of your evidence and the formation of your case.

Stage 2. The main outline

From the patterns of a routine hearing described above, a party's presentation needs to consist of these elements, in this order:

Housekeeping matters – Introduction – Evidence – Submissions – Summary

Now using your preliminary outline, craft your main outline on this model. Whether you are the plaintiff or the respondent, your task is to lead the decision-maker in a series of simple, logical steps to the result you're asking for. Frame your outline to achieve this.

You can leave out the housekeeping matters for the moment, as these will probably arise closer to the hearing. For the introduction you can combine the 'What I want' section of your preliminary outline with its 'Case in a nutshell'. Then shape the 'Facts and evidence' section to guide the decision-maker through the evidence. For the submissions, use the 'Law' and 'Argument' sections, fitting the facts to the legal requirements, and the 'Other party's case'. Then use your 'Summary' to finish the presentation.

How brief or elaborate you make your main outline depends on the complexity of your case and the formality of the court or tribunal involved. For example, an informal court or tribunal that hears the same types of applications day after day might expect a short, to the point presentation. A more formal court may require great attention to detail. Where the decision-maker, the parties and the lawyers are all familiar with the case and its issues, the hearing may move straight into the evidence stage. In any case, still draft your main outline on the same model as that above. And remember to keep it as simple and as clear as possible. The decision-maker will quickly identify any irrelevant or unclear evidence, and you risk testing their patience.

Transforming the preliminary outline into your main outline shouldn't take much time. Play around with the sections and improve the wording and expression wherever possible.

Once you have completed your main outline, check that it is accurate and contains all the necessary elements of your case but no more. Delete any irrelevancies. Check that the points you make follow coherently. Be thorough, but don't make it more complicated than it needs to be.

Here is one example of a main outline of a presentation, using the information from the preliminary outline of Example 2 the plaintiff's case in a consumer matter. Its contents, including the laws and cases, are purely fictional so don't use any of the information in the outline for your own presentation.

MAIN OUTLINE

Example

Plaintiff's case in a consumer matter

THE LAWS AND CASES USED IN THIS EXAMPLE ARE FICTITIOUS. DO NOT USE THEM IN THE PREPARATION OF YOUR CASE.

1 Introduction

Builder's Warranty case. This is a claim against the builder under the provisions of the *House Building Act 2001* for the cost of repairs to the roof of my home to make it habitable. The claim is for $7725 plus $40 filing fee plus interest pursuant to the *Small Claims Act 1993*.

2 Evidence

June–December 2005 Home built by Easy Build Ltd, Builders Licence No 344402. (BUILDING CERTIFICATE DATED DECEMBER 2005)

December 2006 Home purchased by me. (COPY OF CERTIFICATE OF TITLE)

January 2008 Roof began leaking.

January 2008 Letters sent to builder requesting repairs under

Builder's Warranty. (COPY OF TWO LETTERS SENT DATED 4/1/08 AND 28/1/08)

February 2008 Inspection by Office of Fair Trading, rectification order issued to builder. (COPY OF BUILDING REPORT AND RECTIFICATION ORDER DATED 20/2/08) February–May 2008 Problem not rectified. No action taken by builder.

(PHOTOS OF CURRENT STATE OF ROOF AND RAIN DAMAGE TO CEILING, DATED 2/7/08)

15 June 2008 Two quotes obtained for repair of roof. (TWO QUOTES)

1 July 2008 Claim issued.

3 Submissions

Section 20(c) *House Building Act 2001* provides the following warranty for the building of new dwellings: 'a warranty that, if the work consists of the construction of a dwelling, the work will result, to the extent of the work conducted, in a dwelling that is reasonably fit for occupation as a dwelling.' (COPY OF SECTION 20(c))

Section 45 *House Building Act 2001* states: 'The warranty shall be for a period of seven years from the date of completion of construction.' (COPY OF SECTION 45)

The warranty created by the *House Building Act 2001* applies to this home because it is less than seven years since completion of its construction. Under the warranty, the builder is liable to construct a building that's reasonably fit for occupation as a dwelling. The Inspection Report and Rectification Order carried out by the Office of Fair Trading show that the poor construction of the roof has resulted in the home not being reasonably fit for occupation as a dwelling. The builder is liable for repairing the roof.

I have notified the builder of the problem and requested that he fix it. He has not fixed it.

The respondent denies that the damage is due to poor construction. The Inspection Report and the Rectification Order prove that it is.

4 Summary

> My evidence shows I own the home, that it is less than seven years old and it is not reasonably fit for habitation due to the poor construction by the builder. Under the *House Building Act 2001,* the builder is liable.

Witnesses

If you or the other party are using witnesses at the hearing, you'll need to prepare your questions beforehand as part of your presentation.

For your own witnesses, determine exactly what the decision-maker needs from each of them in order to build your case. Pinpoint the relevant facts they can confirm, any doubts or inconsistencies they can clear up and any important gaps or weaknesses they can expose in the other party's case. When examining your own witness, avoid asking leading questions. These are ones that clearly or obviously suggest the answers you want.

For your opponent's witnesses, determine what the decision-maker needs from your cross-examination of each witness in order to cast doubt on your opponent's case. Expose important inconsistencies or weaknesses in their evidence. Target the facts you need to challenge, bearing in mind your own evidence that can support your challenge.

With all witnesses, yours and theirs, make your questions simple and clear. Make them single-barrelled; that is, asking only one thing at a time. Focus on how best to ask a question to extract the information you need. Avoid ambiguity. Avoid questions that elicit information you aren't aware of. The rule 'don't ask a question you don't know the answer to' is a valuable one.

If your witness has made an affidavit or witness statement and you're satisfied that it contains all of their evidence, check with the other party whether they'll be required for cross-examination. If not, check with the court or tribunal whether the witness is needed at the hearing. Sometimes the witness may not need to attend.

If your witness is required to attend, the traditional procedure for them giving evidence is as follows. This method is appropriate for most courts and tribunals. Some informal tribunals, especially those not bound by rules of evidence, accept a more casual approach.

In all cases, instruct your witness to sit outside the court or hearing room until called in and to speak to no-one about their evidence until after they have finished giving it. Also, instruct them beforehand to direct their answers in the witness box to the decision-maker and not to the person asking the questions.

When it's time for your witness to give evidence, the court official will call them into court and swear them in. They can swear an oath or make an affirmation. When this is done, ask them to state their name, address and occupation. After this, begin your questions.

If they have made an affidavit or witness statement, begin your examination-in-chief by presenting it to them and asking them to confirm that they made this affidavit or statement and that it contains their evidence. Then state that you wish to tender this document. Hand it to the court official who will then pass it to the decision-maker. It will be received formally as evidence and given a number or letter, like Exhibit A.

If you're satisfied with its contents and there are no last-minute additions or clarifications, you may have no further questions for your witness. This will end the examination-in-chief and the witness will then be cross-examined by the other party.

If there is extra evidence to obtain from your witness or you want to clarify something in the affidavit, tailor your questions accordingly. Make sure your examination-in-chief covers all the matters you wish to raise with this witness.

If there is no affidavit or witness statement, your examination-in-chief must draw out all the relevant facts that you want this witness to provide. Later on in their evidence, for example during re-examination, you can't raise new matters with this witness unless your opponent has raised them in cross-examination. Also, in examination-in-chief, you can't ask your witness leading questions.

For your opponent's cross-examination of your witness, instruct the witness beforehand not to answer any question that they don't fully understand. If the question is vague or ambiguous, confusing, complicated or the witness doesn't know the meaning of some of the words, tell the witness to ask that the question be explained or rephrased. A witness is also not required to answer a question if the answer might incriminate them. In cross-examination, though, leading questions are allowed.

While your witness is under cross-examination, do not speak to them about how to answer. For example, if there is an adjournment during the cross-examination, be careful not to advise your witness to answer any question in a particular way.

During cross-examination of your witness you can object to your opponent's questioning on much the same grounds as objecting to any other evidence. Check the basic rules of evidence, found in the section 'The facts' in chapter 11 'Preparing your case part 2'.

If you are giving evidence yourself or you're required for cross-examination, follow the same procedure as with any other witness. Go to the witness box and after being sworn in, state your name, address and occupation. State your evidence and then wait to be cross-examined.

With your opponent's witnesses, listen very carefully to the evidence they give during examination-in-chief. Add any new questions you have to your pre-prepared list of questions for your cross-examination.

Successful cross-examination tests the witness's evidence. Could they be wrong? Could they have remembered incorrectly? Could they have a vested interest in remembering incorrectly? Is their evidence as important to your opponent's case as it seems?

When preparing your questions for cross-examination, be careful not to get sidetracked into personal issues. Of course, a witness's credibility should be questioned where appropriate, but nothing useful is gained from mud-slinging and animosity. Your opponent can object to your questions in the same way as objecting to other evidence. Check the rules of evidence again.

When challenging a witness's testimony, you must directly state to that witness your allegations about their evidence. This gives them the opportunity to respond to the allegations. For example you might say: 'I put it to you, that without your glasses on, your eyesight isn't good enough to tell whether it was any white car or my white car.'

Stage 3. The summarised outline

Once you've completed your main outline, you now have all the necessary information of your case arranged in suitable order for the hearing. The final step in preparing your outline is to produce a summarised version to guide you through the complete presentation.

On the day, instead of labouring through your main outline in rote fashion, like reading from a script, have a summarised version beside you to use as a prompt throughout the presentation.

Prepare the summary in point form. Make it easy to follow. Be sure to include the bracketed sections, to indicate which evidence and other paperwork you'll be using and where you'll be using it.

Some of the documents you'll be using as evidence may have already been lodged with the court or tribunal, for example, as part of the claim or defence. For these, mark on your summarised outline where during the course of your presentation you'll draw attention to the relevant parts of them, or if required, formally tender them. For documents that haven't been lodged with the court, mark on your outline where during the hearing you will be tendering them.

Here is an example of how your summarised outline might look. It uses the tenancy example, Example 1, of 'The preliminary outline'. Remember, its contents are fictional so don't use any of the laws or cases in your own case.

SUMMARISED OUTLINE

Example

Plaintiff's case in a tenancy dispute
THE LAWS AND CASES USED IN THIS EXAMPLE ARE FICTITIOUS. DO NOT USE THEM IN THE PREPARATION OF YOUR CASE.

Your case is being heard by an informal tenancy tribunal that deals with similar such cases each day.

1 Introduction

Fair wear and tear case

Claim for $1180 from the $1200 bond

Damage to carpet, curtains and bathroom basin

2 Evidence

Details of tenancy (REFER TO TENANCY AGREEMENT)

Details of condition of premises at start of tenancy (REFER TO CONDITION REPORT)

Details of damage (REFER TO FINAL INSPECTION REPORT)

Extent of damage (TENDER PHOTOS)

Cost of repairs (TENDER ORIGINALS OF QUOTES, LETTERS AND RECEIPTS)

3 Submissions

Clause 20 Tenancy Agreement: Tenants liable except for fair wear and tear.

Smith v Jones case: Age of item is relevant. Here, carpet, curtains and basin are less than 10 years old. (TENDER COPY OF *SMITH V JONES* CASE)

Section 15 *Tenancy Act 1989:* Parties must minimise their loss. Here, the quotes and receipts show I have chosen the lowest quotes to repair the damage. Attempts to repair the carpet were unsuccessful. Replacement is needed.

The premises aren't covered by insurance for this damage.

4 Summary

Damage is not fair wear and tear. Tenants are liable.

Final preparations for the hearing

As the hearing date approaches, make your final preparations. Use a checklist.

Group your outlines together with the necessary documents you're using for the presentation. Order your documents in accordance with your main outline. Number them if necessary. Use post-it notes or post-it flags to be able to find the relevant bits quickly. Highlight the parts you'll be referring to.

Make extra photocopies of any documents that you will be tendering. One copy is for you, one is for the other party and the original is for the decision-maker. If there is more than one decision-maker hearing your case, make a copy for each of them. Also make copies of the cases you'll be using.

Make extra copies of your chronology, one for each decision-maker and one for the other party. This isn't essential, but if you tender a chronology at the beginning of your presentation, it can be a great help to the decision-maker.

Check that you have prepared, filed and served all necessary documents within the required time limits. Check with the court or tribunal how much time has been allotted for your hearing. Assess whether your outline corresponds roughly to half this.

Confirm with your witnesses that they're aware of the hearing date and will attend, where required. Check that they have the correct address of the court or tribunal and correct time of the hearing. Confirm the witness arrangements with the court or tribunal.

If appropriate, continue with attempts to settle the case before the hearing.

If you need to delay the hearing for some serious reason, notify the court or tribunal and the other party as soon as possible. Request an adjournment in writing, stating the reason and your next available time. If possible, get the other party's consent to the adjournment.

Lastly, prepare yourself psychologically for the result. Think through what will happen, win or lose, after the hearing. Investigate and strategically plan for both. For example, if you lose, how much money might you be liable for? How much time might you be given to pay? Will you need extra time to pay? Can you afford to pay in a lump sum or do you need to pay by instalments? Investigate the options and procedures to obtain a suitable arrangement. Make the calculations and be ready to ask at the hearing for these terms to be included in the orders.

Likewise if you win, you might want certain conditions of payment to be included in the orders. You might want other conditions included.

When you represent yourself and win, you can't ask to be awarded legal costs because these relate to the costs of a lawyer and you don't have one. If you lose, though, you may be ordered to pay the legal costs of your opponent's lawyer.

If there's a likelihood of costs being awarded against you, prepare a list beforehand of reasons why you shouldn't have to pay these costs. For instance, if there's an agreement in writing signed by both parties that each will bear their own legal costs, take this agreement with you to the hearing. Or perhaps the other party's lawyer has caused you significant extra effort by unnecessary delays, stalling tactics or general neglect in negotiating or settling the matter earlier. Record these details on your list and attach any relevant paperwork. At the hearing, be prepared to raise this matter at the conclusion of your presentation.

Also make a list of any housekeeping matters that need to be dealt with at the start of the hearing.

You should now have a neat, ordered bundle of documents to take to the hearing.

CHECKLIST OF DOCUMENTS FOR THE HEARING

1 Hearing notice stating the hearing date, time and hearing room or court number;

2 Claim and defence documents;

3 Any other documents filed with the court, for example, affidavits, witness statements;

4 List of any housekeeping matters to be raised at the beginning of the hearing;

5 Copies of chronology;

6 Main outline and summarised outline plus ordered copies of all evidence and cases;

7 List of questions for witnesses (yours and theirs);

8 Any submissions about terms of payment or other terms of the orders;

9 Any submissions about costs;

10 A folder containing all remaining sundry documents, correspondence, notes, drafts, preliminary outline and 'just in case' items;

11 Your diary or a calendar to check dates or confirm a future date if further hearing time is required.

13
The hearing

The hearing is your opportunity to have an impartial decision-maker listen to both sides of the case and then decide it. It is the culmination of your extensive preparations and hopefully the last step towards resolution. It is your chance to have the dispute finalised so that you can move on with your life.

To make the most of this chance, don't approach the hearing with uncertainty and fear. Instead, face it with a clear head and have confidence in yourself, your preparations and your desired outcome.

Here are some practical tips about the hearing day and a final look at the Golden Rules.

What to expect at the hearing

Courtrooms nowadays come in all shapes and sizes. Your case might be heard in a large, traditional courtroom, a small informal one or a meeting room called a hearing room. On the day, it might be devoted to your case alone or there might be hearings in it before and after you.

Most courts are open to the public, so you might have an audience. There might be other parties and their lawyers or Joe Bloggs and his whole family. You might have student groups on school excursions traipsing through. Staff and decision-makers can generally ignore these intrusions. When presenting your case, you'll need to too.

A traditional courtroom looks something like this:

```
                    Decision-maker
      Associate                     Sound recordist
      Witness box                   Court official

                      Bar table
   Parties and the public      Parties and the public
                  Public entrance door
```

The decision-maker sits in an area called the **bench.** The decision-maker, **associate** and sound recordist sit facing the rest of the court.

The associate assists the decision-maker. The sound recordist tapes the proceedings. You can order a copy of the tape or transcript later, but these aren't cheap. They are mainly used if the matter is appealed.

The court official's duties include calling the court to order at the beginning and end of a session, announcing cases, calling witnesses in from outside the courtroom as well as swearing them in. In some courts, the roles of associate, sound recordist and court official are combined and done by just one official.

The lawyers sit at the **Bar table.** When you represent yourself, you usually sit here also.

Behind the Bar table are rows of seats for the public. Where the parties in a case are using lawyers, the parties usually sit here but as near as possible to their lawyers at the Bar table.

Behind the public seating is the entrance door. If you enter or leave the court while the decision-maker is present, you need to bow your head in their direction when you reach the door. A brief nod-type bow will suffice.

A less traditional hearing room might look like this:

```
              Tribunal Member
   You                        Presiding
   Witness                    Member
              Tribunal Member
```

You and a panel of tribunal members might sit around a large table with a seat left vacant for a witness. The Presiding Member will direct the proceedings. This type of hearing is probably closed to the public.

In between these two extremes there are many variations of room arrangements. It's best to investigate or visit the court or hearing rooms beforehand so you know what to expect.

Most court sessions usually start at 10am, then have morning tea about 11am, stop for lunch at 1pm, reconvene at about 2pm and finish for the day at around 4pm. Be aware, some start at 9.30am. Your hearing notice will state what time to be there.

Arrive early. Parking isn't always easy, especially if the court is busy that day. Also it can take considerable time once you're in the building to locate the right court or hearing room. Some court buildings have both courtrooms and hearing rooms. Hearing Room 3, for instance, may not be the same as Courtroom 3. The rooms might not be clearly marked.

If your hearing time is, say, 10am this isn't necessarily when your hearing will start. Although you must be there at 10am, there may be several cases listed ahead of you and you may have to wait your turn. So just in case, bring a newspaper or something to occupy your time. Dress comfortably but in a manner appropriate to the setting. You may be expected to stand to give your presentation and to stand whenever the decision-maker addresses you.

Be sure to address the decision-maker respectfully. A judge is called Your Honour. A magistrate is called Your Worship or Your Honour, depending on which state or territory you're in. A tribunal member is called Tribunal Member or you can add their name, for instance, Tribunal Member Smith. You can also call any of these decision-makers Sir or Madam.

At all times conduct yourself with civility and consideration. This helps maintain an environment of respect between the parties and also respect for the legal system that you're using to resolve your dispute.

Treat your opponent and their lawyer professionally and politely. Very little is ever gained using hostility, and much can be achieved using tact. So don't interrupt them while they're speaking, don't be provoked if they're nasty, refer to them pleasantly, and consider their ideas carefully while at the same time pursuing your competing goal. Each party has an equal right to present their case, and by respecting their job you will be respecting your own.

This professional approach can help your case in several ways. It gets rid of unproductive emotion and keeps the hearing on track towards a workable outcome. It short-circuits attempts to get you off-guard and then anger, intimidate, manipulate or bulldoze you into a position you aren't prepared for. It saves valuable hearing time. And by not buying into trouble you avoid being sidetracked. Behaving well helps keep you focused.

{***Golden Rule of Litigation:*** CONDUCT YOURSELF POLITELY AND PROFESSIONALLY}

Throughout the hearing be simple, clear and direct. Speak naturally and wherever possible use your own words. Be brief and stick to the point.

Being simple means using common everyday words and natural speech to explain yourself clearly. It does not mean oversimplifying your argument. It means breaking down your argument into bite-sized chunks that follow logically and easily to form an idea. Complex arguments that are conveyed simply can be very convincing.

{***Golden Rule of Litigation:*** BE SIMPLE, BE BRIEF}

Every hearing has its surprises. It might be evidence you weren't aware of, a new slant on the law you hadn't thought of, an unexpected development from a witness or a remark from the decision-maker that sheds a different light on the whole case. Or it might be something more practical like a mix-up with the hearing room, misplaced documents, a witness who doesn't turn up, you don't feel well, or you have a bingle beforehand in the car park.

Whatever comes your way on the hearing day, deal with it. Take the time, proceed calmly, and with a minimum of fuss, get on with your case.

{*Golden Rule of Litigation:* EXPECT SURPRISES}

Throughout your presentation, aim to follow your outline as closely as possible. But if circumstances change, be prepared to improvise. If you need a few moments to consider a new development, ask for it. If you need a brief adjournment to examine new evidence, think something through, make revisions or do calculations, ask for it.

If at any time during the hearing you do not understand what's happening, wait for a convenient moment to interrupt, then ask the decision-maker for an explanation. It is crucial that you understand what's going on.

{*Golden Rule of Litigation:* DON'T BE AFRAID TO ASK QUESTIONS}

Finally, if the decision-maker seems hostile, don't take it personally. Do not assume that it's you or your case or the bright shirt you're wearing. You can't possibly know their reason for being out of sorts. If they make opposing remarks, listen to them and respond firmly but courteously then continue presenting your case. Weather the storm.

{***Golden Rule of Litigation:*** IF YOU GET SIDETRACKED, DON'T LOSE YOUR WAY}

{***Golden Rule of Litigation:*** NEVER FORGET WHAT YOU WANT}

Let's look one last time at all of the Golden Rules of Litigation. Use them to recall everything you know about how to run your case.

THE GOLDEN RULES

THE DOs

DO YOUR HOMEWORK; BE PREPARED
KEEP ACCURATE RECORDS

OBEY THE TIME LIMITS FOR LODGING DOCUMENTS
KNOW THE FACTS
CONFIRM THE FACTS WITH EVIDENCE
KNOW THE LAW
KNOW HOW THE LAW APPLIES TO THE FACTS
GET RID OF YOUR EMOTION
CONDUCT YOURSELF POLITELY AND PROFESSIONALLY
IF YOU GET SIDETRACKED, DON'T LOSE YOUR WAY
BE SIMPLE, BE BRIEF
EXPECT SURPRISES

THE DON'Ts

DON'T BE AFRAID TO ASK QUESTIONS
DON'T WASTE TIME ON IRRELEVANCIES
DON'T GET RATTLED, DON'T BE BULLDOZED
NEVER FORGET WHAT YOU WANT

Above all, stay cool and calm. Be yourself. Now off you go to your hearing.

14

The result

The verdict can come in various forms. It can be delivered verbally by the decision-maker at the end of the hearing. It can be reserved, that is, handed down by the decision-maker at a later date. Or you may just receive a copy of the written decision in the mail.

If the decision is delivered verbally, it can happen quite quickly. After giving a brief overview of the facts and then reasons for the decision, the decision-maker may just state the result and the specific orders made.

Decision-makers regularly begin their delivery with positive comments about the losing argument. So what may start out favourably may not end as a favourable result. Wait for the conclusion and don't interrupt the decision-maker during their delivery of the result.

Make sure you understand the orders clearly, especially in terms of what you have to do and what the other party has to do. If you don't understand any part of them, ask the decision-maker at an appropriate moment to explain. If you have any queries, such as about dates of payment or required actions, now is your chance to clear up any potential problems.

Often you can also pick up a copy of the orders at the counter of the registry on your way out. Read these carefully before you leave. Make sure the information in them, especially the names, addresses, any dates of payment and amounts of money, are correct and correspond to what the decision-maker actually said. If there are errors or you have any queries, ask at the registry *before you leave.* It can be quite difficult to have orders changed later.

If the decision is reserved, it may take weeks or even months to find out the result. You will be notified in due course when the decision is to be announced. You might be required to attend court to hear the decision delivered verbally by the decision-maker. Or else a copy of the written decision may be available on the day to be picked up at the counter of the registry.

Often with reserved decisions, the judgment contains the specific orders along with lengthy written reasons for the decision. Read these carefully and seek legal advice if you have any queries. If the query is a practical one, the registry may be able to answer it.

If you receive the written decision in the mail, it may or may not contain the reasons for the result. If it doesn't contain reasons, you may be able to apply for a written statement of reasons. In any event read the decision carefully, get legal advice about any queries and contact the registry if there are any errors.

Winning and losing

In an adversarial system like ours, the result usually produces a winner and a loser. For the winner, it's easy to believe that the result is a good one, that the legal system is a good one, and that justice has prevailed. But for the loser, it can be hard to reconcile a bad result with any notions of fairness and justice.

A better approach to the decision, whether you're the winner or the loser, is to concentrate just on the following:
- what does the result actually mean?
- what are its consequences?
- what are your options?

The result may be either more or less clear-cut than it appears. Wordy, difficult to read decisions can still result in a very clear and practical outcome. Likewise, brief and easy to read orders may have complex ramifications for other aspects of your life. So if you have any trouble understanding the decision or its consequences, get legal advice.

Now investigate your options for compliance with the orders. If you are the unsuccessful party and you're unable to carry out the orders, you may be able to apply to the court or tribunal to have the orders varied or set aside, or to have further orders made regarding payment or other arrangements. There may be provision for financial hardship.

Similarly, if you are the winning party do not assume that compliance with the orders will happen automatically. The other party might be unwilling or unable to comply and you may have to resort to enforcement measures.

For most parties, receiving the result puts an end to the dispute. For better or worse, they accept the verdict, carry out the orders and get on with their lives. For a small proportion though, the matter doesn't end here and the decision is appealed to a higher authority.

If you are the unsuccessful party one of your options may be to appeal the matter. There are time limits for appealing and it is vitally important to appeal within time. Otherwise, you may lose your right to appeal. See the section on 'Appeals'.

If you are the successful party and you suspect your opponent may either not comply or may take the matter further, it is best not to celebrate your victory until either the orders have been carried out, for example, the money is in your hand, or the time limit to appeal has expired.

Enforcement

If you are the successful party and you aren't completely confident that the orders will be carried out, contact the registry and investigate your enforcement options.

If you're the unsuccessful party and you aren't able to comply with the orders, find out the consequences and any alternative courses of action. Look up the legislation, ask at the registry or find out from the website exactly what the court's powers are to change the arrangements and what sanctions you will face for contravening the orders.

If the judgment requires certain action, for instance in some of the family law orders, the possible sanctions for non-compliance may include contempt of court proceedings, a fine or bond or sentence of imprisonment.

If the judgment involves a sum of money and it's not paid by the due date, you may face seizure of your property or a **garnishee order** may be placed on your wages plus extra associated administrative fees. Or you may be required to attend court and be examined regarding your financial situation. Such actions may be avoidable, for instance by an application to pay by instalments.

At this stage of the dispute, it is still crucial for both parties to continue keeping accurate records. A party complying with the orders can quickly correct any errors or misunderstandings by producing the appropriate paperwork that proves the compliance. A party unable to comply can increase their chances if they can show specific evidence of their attempts to comply and why their attempts didn't work. A party seeking enforcement or redress when orders are breached will need specific details of the breaches: the 'what, when, where and how'.

{***Golden Rule of Litigation:*** KEEP ACCURATE RECORDS}

The use of enforcement measures can be distressing for all concerned. Although these measures can mark the true end of the dispute they can often trigger, one last time, the full emotion of the dispute for both parties. If you need to institute them, or they are instituted against you, try to deal with the situation calmly and professionally.

Appeals

If you believe the result is wrong, you may be able to appeal it. The right to appeal, however, is not automatic and various restrictions apply. If you are serious about an appeal, there are several factors you must consider. They are:
- whether appeal is available;
- what restrictions apply to the appeal;
- whether there are valid grounds for appeal;
- the time limit for lodging the appeal application;
- the risks of appeal;
- its prospects of success;
- the likely costs of the appeal;
- whether you will need a lawyer.

Most but not all decisions can be appealed. The rules for appeals are found in the laws that relate to the particular decision, for example the *Family Law Act 1975;* or the laws governing the original court or tribunal; or laws governing the appeal court or tribunal, for example the *Administrative Appeals Act 1975.* If appeal is available, you will have little or no choice about which court or tribunal will hear the appeal.

There may be other restrictions on the appeal. In some cases you must first apply for permission, or **leave to appeal,** from the appeal court or tribunal. Or, appeal might only be available for an error of law in the original decision, not for an error of fact. Also, for some appeals new evidence is not allowed.

Activating an appeal doesn't necessarily put the current verdict on hold. You may need to apply to the original or the appeal court or tribunal for a **stay of proceedings,** which stops the decision being carried out until the outcome of the appeal.

Some kinds of appeal look at the case afresh. Other kinds look at the original decision and see if it was wrong. The original decision might be confirmed or set aside and, in some instances, sent back to the original court or tribunal to be reheard.

To find out your appeal rights begin with the website or registry of the court or tribunal that heard your case. If you have a written decision, this may also contain information about your appeal rights. Find out the specific legislation governing your possible appeal, then try <www.austlii.edu.au> for its exact wording.

It's no use appealing a decision because you think it's unfair or wrong or just plain bad. You must have legally valid grounds for an appeal. You must be able to clearly identify how and where the decision went wrong. For example, was the wrong law applied? How? Was the law applied wrongly to the facts? How? Was the law misinterpreted? How? Although you may have every reason to be disgruntled with the quality of the decision, you will not succeed on appeal unless you have a legally winnable argument.

Strict time limits apply to appeals, so you must think and act quickly. You may have as little as 14 or 28 days to lodge the **notice of appeal** or **application for leave to appeal.** Get legal advice immediately.

Find out as much as you can about a possible appeal. Ask a lot of questions. Is appeal available? What kind of appeal? What are the restrictions? What's the time limit for lodging the appeal? And especially get advice on possible grounds for your appeal and your prospects of success.

Find out what you stand to gain – and what you stand to lose – by appealing. There may be a real risk that the appeal decision might leave you worse off than now.

Assess the likely costs of an appeal. The filing fees of appeal courts can be substantial and might not stop at a one-off filing fee for filing the notice of appeal. Check if any waiver of fees is available. There will also be the hidden costs, things like time, energy, frayed nerves, paperwork, telephone calls, photocopying, witness and other expenses.

The other costs you must factor in are the legal costs of your opponent.

Appeals can be serious affairs and your opponent may enlist expensive lawyers to fight this appeal. Should the appeal fail, you risk being held liable for these costs. Get legal advice about this risk.

An appeal will also escalate the complexity and formality of your case. The procedures will be more elaborate, the requirements more demanding, there'll be more jargon and your opponent's lawyers may be more exacting and aggressive. The legal arguments may be difficult to understand, let alone to argue.

Consider seriously whether you need a specialist lawyer. Investigate your options for the right lawyer at the right price. Shop around. If your case concerns an issue of significant public interest, you may be eligible for a grant of legal aid or be able to enlist the services of a **pro bono,** or free, lawyer through one of the Public Interest Advocacy Centres or Clearing Houses.

On a final note, the appeal process can take considerable time to come to hearing. Preparations can take months, even years depending on the type of appeal. Ask yourself if you have the energy to invest in such a significant period of uncertainty. Are you ready to start the litigation wheel turning again?

With all its variables, the appeal process is still probably the most important element in our legal system. An appeal will take your case to a higher authority. The higher the authority, the more powerful and binding are its decisions and the more far-reaching its effects. It is mostly through appeals that vital changes take place as to how our laws are interpreted and applied. For all the effort, appeals can and do produce real change. A win for you at the appeal stage may mean a win for many others like you. Best of luck.

Glossary of terms

administrative law the law regulating government decisions.

admissible acceptable to the court.

adversarial system a legal system that treats the parties to a case as competing adversaries.

affidavit a written statement sworn or affirmed in the presence of an authorised person.

affidavit of service a sworn or declared statement verifying the delivery of documents.

aggravated damages are not often awarded in Australia; they apply where the injury has been aggravated by the wrongdoer's behaviour, for example, their cruelty.

amended defence a document that amends the original defence.

applicant a party initiating an application to the court.

application a claim or motion to the court or tribunal seeking orders.

application for leave to appeal an application asking for permission to appeal.

application for review an application to the court or tribunal seeking reconsideration of an administrative or other decision.

associate the decision-maker's assistant.

balance of probabilities the civil burden of proof in which the plaintiff must prove that their version of the case is more probable than not.

barrister a lawyer who specialises in court work.

Bar table the table in court where the lawyers sit, or where you sit if you are representing yourself.

bench where the judge or magistrate sits in court.

binding if a decision is binding, the court is compelled to follow it.

burden of proof the obligation to prove the case. In non-criminal litigation, the test used to determine whether the plaintiff has adequately proved their case is the balance of probabilities.

call-over a brief hearing in which a date is set for the final hearing.

case citation a system for identifying a case according to its location in a particular law journal or report.

case management conference a meeting between the parties presided over by a court official.

certificate of readiness a document lodged by a party stating their preparations are complete and their case is ready for hearing.

certified copy a copy of a document that contains a verification by an authorised person that they have seen the original and the copy is a true copy.

certiorari a prerogative writ that orders an inferior court or tribunal or administrative body to produce a written record of proceedings to be reviewed by a higher court.

chamber magistrate a court official who provides free legal advice.

chronology a list of the events of the dispute arranged in date order.

civil law non-criminal law, which gives a remedy to the aggrieved party.

civil litigation non-criminal legal action, a lawsuit.

claimant a party initiating a claim.

common law precedent law, law that comes from cases rather than from legislation.

compensatory damages are awarded to compensate for loss suffered; most damages awarded in Australia are compensatory.

compliance certificate a document lodged by a party indicating that the case is ready for hearing.

conference a meeting between the parties presided over by a court or tribunal official.

counter claim where you admit liability for the original claim but want it offset by an amount you are now claiming.

criminal law the law of crimes, in which the state prosecutes or punishes the offender.

cross-claim where you are denying liability for the original claim and making your own claim.

cross-examination the examination of a witness by the party that did not call the witness.

declaration an equitable remedy that sets out the final state of affairs between the parties; for example, a declaration may set out that a debt is not owed.

default judgment judgment made against the defendant where there has been no defence lodged.

defence the defendant's case or a document that sets out the defendant's case.

defendant the party defending a criminal charge or civil claim made against them, sometimes also called *respondent.*

directions hearing a type of minor hearing in which the court does not decide the final result but directs the parties to do certain things in preparation for the main hearing, and then checks whether the directions have been carried out before scheduling a date for the main hearing.

directions list a list of the court's directions hearings for the day.

disbursements expenses for the case that the lawyer needs to recoup; for example, filing fees, the cost of serving documents, the cost of witness or expert reports and any barrister's fees.

discovery a court process that enables a party to obtain a list of and inspect the documents that the other party will be relying on in their case.

enter an appearance in some cases, a respondent or defendant is required to lodge a form notifying the court that they are defending the action either in person or are represented by a solicitor.

equity a body of judge-made law developed over the years to redress injustice within the legal system.

examination-in-chief the examination of a witness by the party that called the witness.

exemplary damages are not commonly awarded in Australia; they apply to punish the wrongdoer, not just compensate the victim.

extension of time if the time limit for lodging a document expires, you may be able to apply for an extension of time in order to lodge it.

family law law that deals with the breakdown of family relationships.

file to lodge a document with a court or tribunal.

filing fees the fees charged for lodging a document with the court.

FOI laws Freedom of Information laws enabling a person to have access to government records and files.

further and better particulars information requested giving specific details of a claim.

garnishee order an order directing a third person, like an employer or bank manager, to pay the debtor's money (for example, from wages) directly into court or to the person who is owed the money.

general damages awarded in personal injury cases for non-economic loss; for example, pain and suffering and loss of amenity of life.

hearing information form a form lodged by a party providing information that the case is ready for hearing.

inferior court a lower court in the legal system, for example the Magistrates Court.

injunction an equitable remedy that orders certain behaviour; it can require a party to do a certain act but is mostly used to restrain a party from doing a certain act.

inquisitorial system a legal system that treats a case as an inquiry by the decision-maker rather than a contest of competing adversaries presided over by the decision-maker.

interim orders orders made by the court that operate until the outcome of the main hearing, sometimes also called *interlocutory orders.*

interlocutory orders orders by the court that operate until the outcome of the main orders, sometimes also called *interim orders.*

interrogatories legal documents served on or by the other party, containing questions that must be answered as part of the preparation of the case for hearing.

jurisdiction the power of a court.

leave to appeal permission to appeal a decision.

leave to apply out of time permission to make an application although the time limit to lodge the application has expired.

limitation date or ***limitation period*** the time limit for initiating a legal action.

mandamus a prerogative writ that means 'we order'; it orders a public official to carry out their public duty or else give reasons to the court for not doing so.

mediation a dispute resolution process.

mention brief preliminary hearing to determine what the status of the case is; for example, whether it needs to be listed for a directions hearing.

mitigate to minimise a loss.

motion a way of petitioning the court; some legal actions can only be initiated in this way.

motions list a list of the motions coming before the court on that day.

no-costs jurisdiction where a court or tribunal cannot award legal costs to a party.

nominal damages awarded where a wrong has been proved but no loss has resulted.

notice of appeal an appeal application.

notice of discontinuance a document lodged by the plaintiff notifying the court that they are withdrawing the claim.

notice of motion a particular application to the court.

notice of withdrawal a document lodged by the plaintiff notifying the court that they are withdrawing the claim.

plaintiff the party initiating a lawsuit, sometimes also called *applicant* or *claimant.*

precedent a case that is binding on a court when deciding a similar case.

preliminary conference a meeting between the parties presided over by a court official.

prerogative writs a group of remedies that apply in administrative law.

pro bono free, at no cost, done for the general good.

prohibition a prerogative writ that forbids a public official from doing a certain act.

re-examination the questioning again of a witness after examination-in-chief and cross-examination has taken place.

registrar an official of the court with various duties ranging from minor decision-making to processing cases and giving advice.

reserved decision or judgment a decision that is not given at the conclusion of the hearing but is made available at a later date.

respondent the party defending a non-criminal court action taken against them.

rules of evidence the rules that govern whether a piece of evidence is admissible in court.

serve a document deliver the document to the other party or their lawyer.

solicitor a lawyer who does a variety of legal work including wills, conveyancing, giving legal advice and minor court work.

specific damages damages for economic loss, such as medical expenses.

specific performance an equitable remedy that orders a party to a contract to perform that contract.

statement of claim a particular form of claim initiating a civil court action.

statement of facts and contentions a document sometimes required by a tribunal in which a party sets out the facts and the legal contentions of their case.

statement of issues a document sometimes required by a tribunal in which a party states the issues of their case.

statutory declaration a written statement declared in the presence of an authorised person, often a Justice of the Peace. It is similar to an affidavit but does not carry the same weight in a court or tribunal.

stay of proceedings a court order which stops a decision being carried out until the outcome of an appeal or other court action.

strike out application an application by one party to have the other party's application or claim dismissed.

submissions a party's written or oral presentation of their case to the court.

subpoena a court document demanding attendance at court or the delivery of particular documents to court.

summons a court document demanding a person attend court.

superior court a higher court in our legal system; for example, the Supreme Court or High Court.

T docs tribunal documents, the documents provided by the tribunal that contain the relevant documents for your case.

tendering documents presenting the documents to the court during the hearing.

waiver exemption, waiver of fees mean you don't have to pay the fees.

without prejudice without detriment to any existing right or claim.

witness statement a statement signed by a witness outlining the relevant facts of their testimony.

written costs agreement an agreement between you and your lawyer setting out the billing arrangements for the lawyer's work.

Useful resources

List of Australian courts and tribunals

Commonwealth

High Court <www.hcourt.gov.au>
Family Court of Australia <www.familycourt.gov.au>
Federal Court <www.fedcourt.gov.au>
Federal Magistrates Court <www.fmc.gov.au>
Industrial Relations Court of Australia <www.fedcourt.gov.au>
Human Rights and Equal Opportunity Commission <www.humanrights.gov.au>
Administrative Appeals Tribunal <www.aat.gov.au>
Australian Competition Tribunal <www.competitiontribunal.gov.au>
Copyright Tribunal of Australia <www.copyrighttribunal.gov.au>
Defence Force Discipline Appeal Tribunal <www.defenceappeals.gov.au>
Defence Force Remuneration Tribunal <www.dfrt.gov.au>

Federal Police Disciplinary Tribunal <www.fpdt.gov.au>
National Native Title Tribunal <www.nntt.gov.au>
Migration Review Tribunal <www.mrt-rrt.gov.au>
Refugee Review Tribunal <www.mrt-rrt.gov.au>
Social Security Appeals Tribunal <www.ssat.gov.au>

Australian Capital Territory

All contact information for ACT courts and tribunals can be found at: <www.courts.act.gov.au>
ACT Supreme Court
ACT Magistrates Court
Jervis Bay Court
Children's Court
Coroner's Court
ACT Administrative Appeals Tribunal
Credit Tribunal
Discrimination Tribunal
Guardianship & Management of Property Tribunal
Health Professions Tribunal
Mental Health Tribunal

Residential Tenancies Tribunal

New South Wales

Supreme Court <www.lawlink.nsw.gov.au/lawlink/Supre_Court/ll_sc.nsf/pages/SCO-index>
District Court <www.lawlink.nsw.gov.au/dc>
Local Court <www.lawlink.nsw.gov.au/lc>
Chief Industrial Magistrates Court <www.lawlink.nsw.gov.au/cim>
Children's Court <www.lawlink.nsw.gov.au/lawlink/childrens_court/ll_cc.nsf/pages/cc_index>
Coroner's Court <www.lawlink.nsw.gov.au/lawlink/coroners_court/ll_coroners.nsf>
Drug Court <www.lawlink.nsw.gov.au/drugcrt>
Land and Environment Court <www.lawlink.nsw.gov.au/lawlink/lec/ll_lec.nsf/pages/LEC_index>
Youth Drug and Alcohol Court <www.lawlink.nsw.gov.au/youthdrugcourt>
Independent Commission Against Corruption <www.icac.nsw.gov.au>

Industrial Relations Commission <www.lawlink.nsw.gov.au/irc>
Judicial Commission <www.judcom.nsw.gov.au/>
Transport Appeal Boards <www.industrialrelations.nsw.gov.au/tab/index.html>
Administrative Decisions Tribunal <www.lawlink.nsw.gov.au/adt>
Consumer, Trader and Tenancy Tribunal <www.cttt.nsw.gov.au>
Dust Diseases Tribunal <www.lawlink.nsw.gov.au/ddt>
Government and Related Employees Appeal Tribunal <www.> <industrialrelations.nsw.gov.au/great/index.html>
Guardianship Tribunal <www.gt.nsw.gov.au>
Local Government Pecuniary Interest and Disciplinary Tribunal <www.dlg.nsw.gov.au/dlg/dlghome/dlg_CommissionTribunalIndex.aspareaindex+PIT&index+3>
Medical Tribunal ph. (02)9377-5742
Mental Health Review Tribunal <www.mhrt.nsw.gov.au/>
Victims Compensation Tribunal <www.lawlink.nsw.gov.au/vs> Workers

Compensation Commission <www.wcc.nsw.gov.au/default.htm>

Northern Territory

Northern Territory Supreme Court <www.nt.gov.au/ntsc/>
Northern Territory Magistrates Court <www.nt.gov.au/justic/ntmc/>
Local Court <www.nt.gov.au/justic/ntmc/about.shtml>
The Court of Summary Jurisdiction <www.nt.gov.au/justic/ntmc/about.shtml>
Youth Justice Court <www.nt.gov.au/justice/ntmc/about.shtml>
The Community Court <www.nt.gov.au/justic/ntmc/about.shtml>
The Family Matters Court <www.nt.gov.au/justice/ntmc/about.shtml>
The Work Health Court <www.nt.gov.au/justic/ntmc/about.shtml>
Small Claims Court <www.nt.gov.au/justic/ntmc/about.shtml>
Anti-Discrimination Commission <www.nt.gov.au/justice/adc/index800.html>
Northern Territory Mental Health Review Tribunal <www.nt.gov.au/justice/courtsupp/mentalhealth/index.shtml>

Northern Territory Lands and Mining Tribunal <www.nt.gov.au/justic/courtsupp/landplantrib/index.shtml>

Queensland

Queensland Supreme Court <www.courts.qld.gov.au/1504.htm>
Queensland District Court <www.courts.qld.gov.au/121/htm>
Queensland Magistrates Court <www.courts.qld.gov.au/126.htm>
Planning and Environment Court <www.courts.qld.gov.au/996.htm>
Industrial Court of Queensland <www.qirc.qld.gov.au>
Queensland Coroners Court <www.courts.qld.gov.au/129.htm>
Land Court of Queensland <www.landcourt.qld.gov.au>
Queensland Industrial Relations Commission <www.qirc.qld.gov.au/index.htm>
Anti-Discrimination Tribunal <www.adcq.qld.gov.au/tribunal/tribunalhome.html>
Health Practitioners Tribunal <www.courts.qld.gov.au/135.htm>

Land and Resources Tribunal of Queensland <www.lrt.qld.gov.au>
Queensland Consumer and Commercial Tribunal <www.tribunals.qld.gov.au>
Queensland Guardianship and Administration Tribunal <www.justice.qld.gov.au/1336.htm>
Children's Services Tribunal <www.justice.qld.gov.au/1753.html>
Legal Practitioners Tribunal <www.courts.qld.gov.au/134.htmld.gov.au/134.htm>
Racing Appeals Tribunal of Queensland <www.tribunals.qld.gov.au>
Small Claims Tribunal <www.courts.qld.gov.au/136.htm>

South Australia

Supreme Court <www.courts.sa.gov.au/courts/supreme/index.html>
District Court <www.courts.sa.gov.au/courts/district/index.html>
Magistrates Court <www.courts.sa.gov.au/courts/magistrates/index.html>
Coroner's Court <www.courts.sa.gov.au/courts/coroner/index.html>

Drug Court <www.courts.sa.gov.au/drug_court/index.html>
Environment Resources and Development Court <www.courts.sa.gov.au/courts/>
Family Violence Court <www.courts.sa.gov.au/magistrates/index.html>
Industrial Relations Court <www.courts.sa.gov.au/courts/industrial/index.html> and <www.industrialcourt.sa.gov.au>
Youth Court <www.courts.sa.gov.au/courts/youth/index.html>
Equal Opportunity Tribunal of South Australia <www.courts.sa.gov.au/courts/district/equal_opportunity_tribunal.htmm>
South Australian Residential Tenancies Tribunal <www.agd.sa.gov.au/services/tribunals.php>
South Australian Workers Compensation Tribunal <www.industrialcourt.sa.gov.au/>
South Australian Workers Compensation Appeal Tribunal <www.industrialcourt.sa.gov.au/>
South Australian Industrial Relations Commission <www.industrialcourt.sa.gov.au/>

Guardianship Board <www.guardianshipboard.sa.gov.au>
Remuneration Tribunal of South Australia <www.remtribunal.sa.gov.au>
Medical Professional Conduct Tribunal <www.courts.sa.gov.au/courts/district/index.html>
Dental Professional Conduct Tribunal <www.courts.sa.gov.au/courts/district/index.html>
Pastoral Land Appeal Tribunal <www.courts.sa.gov.au/courts/district/appeals_and_tribunals.html>
Police Disciplinary Tribunal <www.courts.sa.gov.au/courts/district/appeals_and_tribunals.html>
Warden's Court <www.courts.sa.gov.au/courts/district/appeals_and_tribunals.html>
Soil Conservation Appeal Tribunal <www.courts.sa.gov.au/courts/district/appeals_and_tribunals.html>
Fire Service Appeals <www.courts.sa.gov.au/courts/district/appeals_and_tribunals.html>

Tasmania

Supreme Court <www.supremecourt.tas.gov.au/home>

Magistrates Court <www.magistratescourt.tas.gov.au/home>

Anti-Discrimination Tribunal <www.magistratescourt.tas.gov.au/divisions/Anti-Discrimination_Tribunal>

Mental Health Tribunal <www.mentalhealthtribunal.tas.gov.au/home>

Mining Tribunal <www.magistratescourt.tas.gov.au/divisions/mining_tribunal>

Motor Accidents Compensation Tribunal <www.magistratescourt.tas.gov.au/divisions/motor_accidents_compensation_tribunal>

Resource Management and Planning Appeal Tribunal <www.rmpat.tas.gov.au>

Tasmanian Industrial Commission <www.tic.tas.gov.au>

Workers Rehabilitation and Compensation Tribunal <www.workerscomp.tas.gov.au>

Victoria

Supreme Court of Victoria <www.supremecourt.vic.gov.au>

Magistrates Court of Victoria <www.magistratescourt.vic.gov.au>

Children's Court of Victoria <www.childrenscourt.vic.gov.au>

County Court of Victoria <www.countycourt.vic.gov.au>

Drug Court <www.magistratescourt.vic.gov.au>

State Coroner's Office of Victoria <www.coronerscourt.vic.gov.au>

Municipal Electoral Tribunal <www.magistratescourt.vic.gov.au>

Family Violence Court Division <www.magistratescourt.vic.gov.au>

Koori Court <www.magistratescourt.vic.gov.au>

Neighbourhood Justice Centres <www.justice.vic.gov.au>

Victims of Crime Assistance Tribunal <www.vocat.vic.gov.au>

Victorian Civil and Administrative Tribunal <www.vcat.vic.gov.au>

Victorian Mental Health Review Board <www.mhrb.vic.gov.au>

Western Australia

Supreme Court <www.supremecourt.wa.gov.au>
District Court <www.districtcourt.wa.gov.au>
Magistrates Court <www.magistratescourt.wa.gov.au>
Aboriginal Community Court <www.justice.wa.gov.au>
Children's Court <www.justice.wa.gov.au>
Drug Court <www.justice.gov.wa.au>
Family Court of Western Australia <www.familycourt.wa.gov.au>
Family Violence Court <www.justice.wa.gov.au>
Liquor Licensing Court <www.justice.wa.gov.au>

Office of the State Coroner <www.coronerscourt.wa.gov.au> Prisons Review Board <www.prisonersreviewboard.wa.gov.au> Supervised Release Review Board <www.justice.wa.gov.au> Mentally Impaired Accused Review Board <www.justice.wa.gov.au> State Administrative Tribunal <www.sat.justice.wa.gov.au>

Western Australian Industrial Relations Commission <www.wairc.wa.gov.au>

Dispute resolution services

These agencies offer dispute resolution services as an alternative to going to court:

ACT Conflict Resolution Service ph. (02)6162-4050

Centacare – mediation for separating and divorcing couples ph. 1300-364-277

NSW Community Justice Centres ph. 1800-990-777

NSW Retail Tenancy Unit – for commercial lessors and lessees ph. 1300-795-534

Northern Territory Community Justice Centres ph. 1800-000-473

Queensland Dispute Resolution Branch ph. 1800-017-288

Relationships Australia – relationship counselling ph.1300-364-277

Tasmania Positive Solutions ph.
1800-664-20

Unifam – NSW/ACT family counselling
and mediation ph. (02)9373-5500

Victoria Dispute Settlement Centre ph.
1800-658-528

Western Australia Aboriginal Alternative
Dispute Resolution Service ph.
1800-045-577

For communications industry complaints:
Telecommunications Industry
 Ombudsman ph. 1800-062-058
Postal Industry Ombudsman ph.
 1300-362-072

For electricity, gas and water complaints:
Energy and Water Ombudsman NSW
 ph. 1800-246-545
Energy and Water Ombudsman Victoria
 ph. 1800-500-09
Energy Industry Ombudsman South
 Australia ph. 1800-665-565

Energy Ombudsman Queensland ph. 1800-662-837
Energy Ombudsman Tasmania ph. 1800-001-170
Energy Ombudsman Western Australia ph. 1800-754-004

For financial services complaints:
Financial Ombudsman Service ph. 1300-780-808

(includes Banking and Financial Services Ombudsman, Credit Ombudsman Service, Credit Union Dispute Resolution Centre, Financial Co-operative Dispute Resolution Scheme, Financial Industry Complaints Service,

Insurance Brokers Disputes Limited, Insurance Ombudsman Service, Superannuation Complaints Tribunal)

For complaints about public and private health services:
Private Health Insurance Ombudsman ph. 1800-640-695

ACT Health Services Commissioner ph.
(02)6205-2222

NSW Health Care Complaints
Commission ph. (02)9219-7444-or
1800-043-159

NT Health and Community Services
Complaints Commission ph.
1300-766-725

Qld Health Quality & Complaints
Commission ph. (07)3234-0272-or
1800-077-308

SA Health & Community Services
Complaints Commissioner ph.
(08)8226-8666-or 1800-232-007

Tasmanian Health Complaints
Commissioner ph. 1300-766-725

Victorian Office of the Health Services
Commissioner ph. (03)8601-5200-or
1800-136-066

WA Office of Health Review ph.
(08)9323-0600-or 1800-813-583

For complaints against government departments and agencies:
Commonwealth Ombudsman ph. 1300-362-072
(includes Defence Force Ombudsman, Immigration Ombudsman, Law Enforcement Ombudsman, Postal Industry Ombudsman and Taxation Ombudsman)
ACT Ombudsman ph. (02)6276-0111
New South Wales Ombudsman ph. (02)9286-1000 or 1800-451-524
Northern Territory Ombudsman ph. (08)8999-1818-or 1800-806-380
Queensland Ombudsman ph. (07)3005-7000 or 1800-068-908
South Australian Ombudsman ph. (08)8226-8699-or 1800-182-150
Tasmanian Ombudsman ph. (03)6233-6217 or 1800-001-170
Victorian Ombudsman ph. (03)9613-6222 or 1800-806-314
(includes the Victorian Public Transport Ombudsman)
WA Ombudsman ph. (08)9220-7555 or 1800-117-000

Legal aid

National Legal Aid

<www.nla.aust.net.au>

Australian Capital Territory

<www.legalaid.canberra.net.au>

Telephone advice ph. 1300-654-314-After Hours Legal Advice ph. 0429-440-084-Local office ph. (02)624-33471

New South Wales

<www.legalaid.nsw.gov.au>
Law Access (for free information, advice and referral) ph. 1300-888-529
Legal Aid Youth Hotline ph. 1800-101-810

Sydney metropolitan offices:
City Head Office ph. (02)9219-5000
Bankstown ph. (02)9707-4555
Blacktown ph. (02)9621-4800
Burwood ph. (02)9747-6155
Campbelltown ph. (02)4628-2922

Fairfield ph. (02)9727-3777
Liverpool ph. (02)9601-1200
Manly ph. (02)9977-1479
Parramatta (civil and family law) ph.
 (02)9891-1600
Penrith ph. (02)4732-3077
Sutherland ph. (02)9521-3733

NSW regional:
Coffs Harbour ph. (02)6651-7899
Dubbo ph. (02)6885-4233
Gosford ph. (02)4324-5611
Lismore ph. (02)6621-2082
Newcastle ph. (02)4929-5482
Nowra ph. (02)4422-4351
Orange ph. (02)6362-8022
Tamworth ph. (02)6766-6322
Wagga Wagga ph. (02)6921-6588
Wollongong ph. (02)4228-8299

Northern Territory

<www.ntlac.nt.gov.au>
Legal Information Line ph.
 1800-019-343
To attend for an appointment with a
 solicitor at the Civil Law Clinic at

Darwin or Palmerston ph.
(08)8999-3000

Head office:
Darwin ph. (08)8999-3000

Regional offices:
Alice Springs ph. (08)8951-5377
Katherine ph. (08)8973-8704
Palmerston ph. (08)8999-4750
Tennant Creek ph. (08)8962-1985

Queensland

<www.legalaid.qld.gov.au>
Free Legal Information and Civil Law
 Legal Aid Scheme ph. 1300-65-1188

South Australia

<www.lsc.sa.gov.au>
Legal Helpline ph. 1300-366-424
For general inquiries and to make an
 appointment for face-to-face advice
ph. (08)8463-3555
Family Law Duty Lawyer Service ph.
 0434-079-387-or 0434-079-388

Youth Legal Service ph. (08)8463-3533

Regional offices:
Elizabeth ph. (08)8207-9292
Holden Hill ph. (08)8369-1044
Mount Barker ph. (08)8226-8722
Noarlunga ph. (08)8207-3877
Port Adelaide ph. (08)8207-6276
Port Augusta ph. (08)8648-5180
Whyalla ph. (08)8648-8060

Tasmania

<www.legalaid.tas.gov.au> For civil matters contact Telephone Advice Line ph. 1300-366-611

Victoria

<www.legalaid.vic.gov.au>
Victorian Legal Aid Legal Information Service ph. (03)9269-0120-or 1800-677-402

Melbourne offices:
City ph. (03)9269-0234
Broadmeadows ph. (03)9302-8777
Dandenong ph. (03)9767-7111
Frankston ph. (03)9784-5222

Preston ph. (03)9416-6444
Ringwood ph. (03)9259-5444
Sunshine ph. (03)9300-5333

Regional offices:
Ballarat ph. (03)5329-6222
Bairnsdale ph. (03)5153-1975
Bendigo ph. (03)5448-2333-or
 1800-254-500
Geelong ph. (03)5226-5666-or
 1800-196-200
Horsham ph. (03)5381-6000-or
 1800-177-638
Morwell ph. (03)5134-8055
Shepparton (03)5823-6200

Western Australia

<www.legalaid.wa.gov.au>
Infoline ph. 1300-650-579-for general legal advice and information or to make an appointment.
For more detailed advice and help from a solicitor available at a small fee, contact a local office.

Head office:
Perth ph. (08)9261-6222

Regional offices:
Christmas/Cocos Islands ph.
 (08)9164-7529
East Kimberley Region ph.
 (08)9166-5800
Fremantle Region ph. (08)9335-7108
Goldfields Region ph. (08)9091-3255
Great Southern Region ph.
 (08)9892-9700
Midland Region ph. (08)9274-3327
Midwest and Gascoyne Region ph.
 (08)9921-0200
Pilbara Region ph. (08)9172-3733
Southwest Region ph. (08)9721-2277
West Kimberley Region ph.
 (08)9192-1888

Community legal centres

National office

National Association of Community Legal Centres <www.naclc.org.au>

Australian Capital Territory

Consumer Law Centre of the ACT ph. (02)6257-1788<www.carefc.org.au>

Disability Discrimination Legal Service (ACT) ph. (02)6247-2018<www.welfarerightsact.org.au>

Environmental Defender's Office (ACT) Inc. ph. (02)6247-9420<www.edo.org.au/edoact/>

Tenants Union (ACT) ph. (02)6247-2011<www.tenants.org.au>

Welfare Rights and Legal Centre (ACT) ph. (02)6247-2177<www.welfarerightsact.org.au>

Women's Legal Centre (ACT & Region) ph. (02)06257-4499

New South Wales

Aged Care Rights Service ph. (02)9281-3600<www.tars.com.au>

Arts Law Centre of Australia ph. (02)9356-2566<www.artslaw.com.au>

Central Coast Legal Centre ph. (02)4353-4988<www.cclegal.org.au>

Combined Community Legal Centres Group (NSW) Inc. ph. (02)9212-7333<www.nswclc.org.au>

Community Legal Service (Albury Wodonga) ph. (02)6056-8210<www.communitylaw.org.au/alburywodonga>

Consumer Credit Legal Centre (NSW) ph. 1800-808-488<www.cclcnsw.org.au>

Court Support Scheme ph. (02)9288-8700<www.crcnsw.org.au>

Disability Discrimination Legal Centre (NSW) ph. (02)9310-7722<www.ddlcnsw.org.au>

Elizabeth Evatt Community Legal Centre ph. (02)4782-4155<www.eelc.org.au>

Environmental Defender's Office (NSW) ph. (02)9262-6989<www.edo.org.au/edonsw>

Far West Community Legal Centre Inc. ph. (08)8088-2020<www.farwestclc.org.au>

Hawkesbury Nepean Community Legal Centre ph. (02)4588-5618

HIV/AIDS Legal Centre (NSW) ph. (02)9206-2060<www.halc.org.au>

Hunter Community Legal Centre ph. (02)4926-3220

Illawarra Legal Centre ph. (02)4276-1939<www.illawarralegalcentre.org.au>

Immigration Advice and Rights Centre ph. (02)9262-3833

Inner City Legal Centre ph. (02)9332-1966<www.iclc.org.au>

Intellectual Disability Rights Service and Criminal Justice Support Network ph. (02)9318-0144<www.idrs.org.au>

Kingsford Legal Centre ph. (02)9385-9566<www.kingsfordlegalcentre.org>

Macarthur Legal Centre ph. (02)4628-2042www.macarthurlegal.org.au

Macquarie Legal Centre ph. (02)9760-0111<www.macquarielegal.org.au>

Marrickville Legal Centre ph. (02)9559-2899<www.mlc.asn.au>

Mt Druitt & Area Community Legal Centre ph. (02)9675-2009

National Children's and Youth Law Centre ph. (02)9385-9588<www.lawstuff.org.au> and <www.ncylc.org.au>

National Pro Bono Resource Centre ph. (02)9385-7381<www.nationalprobono.org.au>

North & North West Community Legal Service ph. 1800-687-687<www.communitylegalcentre.websyte.com.au>

Northern Rivers Community Legal Centre ph. (02)6621-1000

Public Interest Advocacy Centre ph. (02)8898-6500<www.piac.asn.au>

Public Interest Law Clearing House ph. (02)8898-6500

Redfern Legal Centre ph. (02)9698-7277<www.rlc.org.au>

Refugee Advice and Casework Service ph. (02)9211-4001<www.racs.org.au>

Shoalcoast Community Legal Centre ph. (02)4422-9529<www.shoalcoast.org.au>

South West Sydney Legal Centre ph. (02)9601-7777<www.swslc.org.au>

Tenants Union of NSW ph. (02)8177-3750<www.tenants.org.au>

Thiyama-Li Family Violence Service (02)6751-1400

University of Newcastle Legal Centre ph. (02)4921-8666<www.newcastle.edu/school/law/unlc.html>

UTS Community Law Centre ph. (02)9514-2914<www.law.uts.edu.au/clc>

Welfare Rights Centre (NSW) ph. (02)9211-5300<www.welfarerights.org.au>

Western NSW Community Legal Centre Inc. ph. (02)6884-9422

Wirringa Baiya Aboriginal Women's Legal Centre ph. (02)9569-3847<www.wirringabaiya.org.au>

Women's Legal Services Limited (NSW) ph. (02)9749-5533<www.womenslegalnsw.asn.au>

Northern Territory

Central Australian Women's Legal Service Inc. ph. (08)8952-4055

Darwin Community Legal Service ph. 1800-812-953<www.dcls.org.au>

Domestic Violence Legal Service ph. (08)8952-1391

Environmental Defenders Office (NT) ph. (08)8982-1182<www.edo.org.au/edont>

Katherine Women's Information & Legal Service (KWILS) ph. (08)8972-1712

North Australian Aboriginal Family Violence Legal Service ph. (08)8923-8200

Top End Women's Legal Service ph. (08)8982-3000

Queensland

Aboriginal and Torres Strait Islander Women's Legal and Advocacy Service ph. (07)3392-3177<www.atsiwlas.org.au>

Aboriginal and Torres Strait Islander Women's Legal Services North Queensland ph. (07)4721-6007

Advocacy and Support Centre ph. (07)4616-9700<www.tascinc.org.au>

Arts Law Centre of Queensland Inc. ph. (07)3211-3628<www.artslawqld.org.au>

Bayside Community Legal Centre ph. (07)3206-2724

Cairns Community Legal Centre ph. (07)4031-7688<www.cclc.org.au>

Care Goondiwindi Association Inc. (07)4670-0700<www.caregoondiwindi.org.au>

Caxton Legal Centre ph. (07)3254-1811<www.caxton.org.au>

Central Queensland Community Legal Centre ph. (07)4922-1200<www.cqclc.org.au>

Citizen's Advice Bureau and Highway Legal Service – Gold Coast Inc. ph. (07)5532-9211<www.advicebureau.org.au>

Disability Discrimination Legal Service ph. 1800-650-197<www.cclc.org.au>

Environmental Defenders Office (Qld) Inc. ph. (07)3211-4466<www.edo.org.au/edoqld>

Environmental Defenders Office of Northern Queensland Inc. ph. (07)4031-4766

Indigenous Family Violence Legal Outreach Unit ph. 1800-142-405

Logan Legal Advice Centre ph. (07)3290-4199<www.yfs.org.au/legaladvice>

Logan Youth Legal Service ph. (07)3208-8199<www.yfs.org.au/legal>

Mackay Regional Community Legal Centre Inc. ph. (07)4953-1211<www.mrclc.com.au>

North Queensland Women's Legal Service – Cairns office ph. (07)4041-0066<www.nqwls.com.au>

North Queensland Women's Legal Service – Townsville office ph. (07)4772-5400<www.nqwls.com.au>

Nundah Community Legal Service ph. (07)3260-6820

Peninsula Community Legal Service (Qld) ph. (07)3284-4543

Pine Rivers Community Legal Service ph. (07)3205-2955<www.prnc.org.au>

Prisoners Legal Service ph. (07)3846-5074<www.plsqld.com>

Queensland Advocacy Inc. ph. (07)3236-1122<www.qai.org.au>

Queensland Association of Independent Legal Services ph. (07)3392-0644<www.qails.org.au>

Queensland Public Interest Law Clearing House Inc. ph. (07)3012-9773<www.qpilch.org.au>

Refugee & Immigration Legal Service Inc. ph. (07)3846-3189<www.rails.org.au>

Roma Community Legal Service Inc. ph. (07)4622-4547

South West Brisbane Community Legal Centre Inc. ph. (07)3372-7677<www.swbcls.org.au>

Stanthorpe Community Legal Service ph (07)4681-3777

Suncoast Community Legal Service Inc. ph. (07)5443-7827

Taylor Street Community Legal Centre ph. (07)4194-6600

Tenants Union of Queensland Inc. ph. (07)3257-1108<www.tuq.org.au>

Tenants Union of Queensland – North Queensland office ph. (07)4031-3194<www.tuq.org.au>

Townsville Community Legal Service Inc. ph. (07)4721-5511

Welfare Rights Centre Inc. (Qld) ph. (07)3421-2510<www.wrcqld.org.au>

Women's Legal Service (Qld) ph. (07)3392-0670<www.wlsq.org.au>

Youth Advocacy Centre ph. (07)3857-1155<www.yac.net.au>

South Australia

Ceduna Aboriginal Family Violence Prevention Legal Service ph. (08)8625-3800

Central Community Legal Service ph. (08)8342-1800<www.ucwesleyadelaide.org.au/ccls>

Children's and Youth Legal Service of South Australia ph. (08)8342-1800<www.ucwesleyadelaide.org.au/ccls/children_youth.htm>

Disability Discrimination Service ph. (08)8342-1800<www.wesleyadelaide.org.au/ccls/disability_discrimination.htm>

Environmental Defenders Office (SA) ph. (08)8410-3833<www.edo.org.au/edosa>

Northern Community Legal Service ph. (08)8281-6911

Refugee Advocacy Service of South Australia Inc. ph. (08)8223-5088

Riverland Community Legal Service Inc. ph. (08)8582-2255

Roma Mitchell Community Legal Centre and Roma Mitchell Human Rights Volunteer Service ph. (08)8362-1199<http://rmhrvs.auspics.org>

South East Community Legal Service Inc. ph (08)8723-6236

Southern Community Justice Centre ph. (08)8384-5222

Warndu Wathilli-Carri Ngura Aboriginal Family Violence Legal Service ph. (08)8641-2195

Welfare Rights Centre (SA) ph. (08)8226-4123<www.wrcsa.org.au>

WestSide Lawyers – Hindmarsh ph. (08)8243-5521<www.westsidelawyers.net>

WestSide Lawyers – Westwood ph. (08)8243-5521<www.westsidelawyers.net>

Women's Legal Service (SA) ph. (08)8221-5553<www.wlssa.org.au>

Women's Legal Service (SA) – Port Augusta office (08)8641-3366<www.wlssa.org.au>

Tasmania

Environmental Defenders Office (Tasmania) Inc. ph. (03)6223-2770<www.edo.org.au/edotas>

Hobart Community Legal Service ph. (03)6223-2500<www.hobartlegal.org.au>

Launceston Community Legal Centre ph. 1800-066-019

North West Community Legal Centre Inc. ph. (03)6426-8720

Tenants Union of Tasmania ph. (03)6223-2641<www.tutas.org.au>

Women's Legal Service (Tas) ph. 1800-682-468<www.womenslegaltas.org.au>

Victoria

Aboriginal and Torres Strait Islander Family Violence Prevention & Legal Service (Vic) ph. (03)9654-3111-or 1800-105-303<www.fvpls.org>

Asylum Seeker Resource Centre ph. (03)9326-6066<www.asrc.org.au>

Brimbank/Melton Community Legal Centre ph. (03)9363-1811<www.communitywest.org.au>

Broadmeadows Community Legal Service ph. (03)9302-3911

Casey Cardinia Community Legal Service ph. (03)9793-1993

Central Highlands Community Legal Centre ph. (03)5331-5999<www.chclc.org.au>

Communications Law Centre ph. (03)9600-3841<www.comslaw.org.au> or <www.oznetlaw.net>

Community Legal Service (Albury Wodonga) ph. (02)6056-8210<www.communitylaw.org.au/alburywodonga>

Consumer Action Law Centre ph. (03)9629-6300<www.consumeraction.org.au>

DEAC Legal Services ph. (03)9655-1117<www.deac.org.au>

Darebin Community Legal Centre ph. (03)9484-7753<www.communitylaw.org.au/darebin>

Disability Discrimination Legal Service Inc. (Vic) ph. (03)9654-8644<www.communitylaw.org.au/ddls>

Eastern Community Legal Centre – Inner East branch ph. (03)9285-4822<www.eclc.org.au>

Eastern Community Legal Centre – Outer East branch ph. (03)9762-6235<www.eclc.org.au>

Environmental Defenders Office (Vic) Ltd ph. (03)8341-3100<www.edo.org.au/edovic>

Essendon Community Legal Centre Inc. ph. (03)9376-7929<www.essclc.org.au>

Family Mediation Centre ph. (03)9556-5333<www.mediation.com.au>

Federation of CLCs (Victoria) Inc. ph. (03)9652-1500<www.communitylaw.org.au>

Fitzroy Legal Service ph. (03)9419-3744<www.fitzroy-legal.org.au>

Flemington & Kensington Community Legal Centre ph. (03)9376-4355<www.communitylaw.org.au>

Footscray Community Legal Centre ph. (03)9689-8444<www.communitylaw.org.au/footscray>

Geelong Community Legal Service ph. (03)5221-4744<www.communitylaw.org.au/geelong>

Gippsland Community Legal Service ph. (03)5133-0411<www.communitylaw.org.au/gippsland>

Human Rights Law Resource Centre Ltd ph. (03)9225-6695<www.hrlrc.org.au>

Job Watch Inc. ph. (03)9662-1933<www.job-watch.org.au>

MAC – Indigenous Family Violence Prevention Legal Service ph. (03)5022-1852

Mental Health Legal Centre ph. (03)9629-4422<www.communitylaw.org.au/mentalhealth/>

Monash Oakleigh Legal Service ph. (03)9905-4336<www.communitylaw.org.au/monashoakleigh>

MU Student Union Legal Service ph. (03)8344-8687<www.union.unimelb.edu.au>

Murray Mallee Community Legal Service ph. (03)5023-5966<www.malleefamilycare.com.au>

North Melbourne Legal Service ph. (03)9328-1885<www.communitylaw.org.au/northmelbourne>

Peninsula Community Legal Centre (Vic) ph. (03)9783-3600<www.communitylaw.org.au/peninsula>

Peninsula Community Legal Centre (Vic) – Bentleigh branch office ph. (03)9570-8455

Peninsula Community Legal Centre (Vic) – Cranbourne branch office

Peninsula Community Legal Centre (Vic) – Pines branch office ph. (03)9783-3600

Public Interest Law Clearing House (Vic) Inc. ph. (03)9225-6680<www.pilch.org.au>

Refugee and Immigration Legal Centre ph. (03)9483-1140<www.rilc.org.au>

St Kilda Legal Service ph. (03)9534-0777

South West Community Legal Centre – Community Connections ph. 1300-361-680<www.comconnect.com.au>

SouthPort Community Legal Service ph. (03)9690-9144

Springvale Monash Legal Service Inc. ph. (03)9562-3144<www.smls.com.au>

Student Legal Service ph. (03)9479-1469

Tenants Union of Victoria ph. (03)9416-2577<www.tuv.org.au>

Victorian Aboriginal Legal Service Cooperative Ltd ph. (03)9419-3888<www.vals.org.au>

Villamanta Disability Rights Legal Service Inc. ph. (03)5229-2925<www.villamanta.org.au>

Welfare Rights Unit (Vic) ph. (03)9416-1111<www.welfarerights.org.au>

West Heidelberg Community Legal Service ph. (03)9450-2002

Western Suburbs Legal Service Inc. ph. (03)9391-2244<www.communitylaw.org.au/westernsuburbs>

Whittlesea Community Legal Service (Whittlesea Community Connections) ph. (03)9401-6655<www.whittleseacommunityconnections.org.au>

Women's Legal Service Victoria ph. (03)9642-0877-or 1800-133-302

Wyndham Legal Service ph. (03)9741-0198<www.communitylaw.org.au/wyndham>

Youthlaw (Vic) ph. (03)9611-2412<www.youthlaw.asn.au>

Western Australia

Albany Community Legal Centre Inc. ph. (08)9842-8566

Armadale Information and Referral Service Inc. ph. (08)9497-1406

Bunbury Community Legal Centre ph. (08)9791-3206

CASE for Refugees ph. (08)9227-7311

Citizens Advice Bureau ph. (08)9221-5711<www.cabwa.com.au>

Community Legal Centres Association (WA) Inc. ph. (08)9221-9322<www.communitylaw.net>

Consumer Credit Legal Service (WA) ph. (08)9221-7066

Employment Law Centre of Western Australia Inc. ph. 1300-130-956

Environmental Defenders Office (WA) ph. (08)9221-3030<www.edowa.org.au>

Fremantle Community Legal Centre ph. (08)9432-9790<www.freofocus.com.au>

Geraldton Family Advocacy Service/Yamatji Family Violence Prevention Legal Unit ph. (08)9965-4654

Geraldton Resource Centre ph. (08)9964-3533<www.grc.asn.au>

Goldfields Community Legal Centre ph. (08)9021-1888-or 1300-139-188

Gosnells Community Legal Centre Inc. ph. (08)9398-1455<www.gosclc.com.au>

Kimberley Community Legal Services Inc. ph. (08)9169-3100

Marninwarntikura Fitzroy Women's Resource Centre ph. (08)9191-5284

Mental Health Law Centre ph. (08)9328-8266<www.mhlcwa.org.au>

Midland Information, Debt and Legal Advocacy Service Inc. ph. (08)9250-2123

Multicultural Services Centre of WA Inc. ph. (08)9328-2699

Northern Suburbs Community Legal Centre ph. (08)9440-1663

Peel Community Legal Service Inc. ph. (08)9581-4511<www.peelclc.com.au>

Pilbara Community Legal Service ph. (08)9140-1613

Pilbara Community Legal Service – Karratha branch office ph. (08)9185-5899

Pilbara Community Legal Service –
Newman branch office ph.
(08)9177-8708

Pilbara Community Legal Service –
Roebourne branch office ph.
(08)9182-1169

Southern Communities Advocacy Legal & Education Service (SCALES) ph. (08)9528-6077<www.law.murdoch.edu/scales>

Sussex Street Community Law Service Inc. ph. (08)9470-2676<www.sscls.asn.au>

Tenants Advice Service Inc. ph. (08)9221-0088<www.taswa.org>

Welfare Rights & Advocacy Service (WA) ph. (08)9328-1751<www.wraswa.org.au>

Women's Law Centre of WA ph. (08)9272-8800

Youth Legal Service ph. (08)9202-1688<
www.youthlegalserviceinc.com.augalser
viceinc.co>

Public law libraries

New South Wales

LIAC (Legal Information Access Centre), State Library, Macquarie Street, Sydney ph. (02)9273-1558

Tasmania

Andrew Inglis Clark Law Library, Lower Ground Floor, Supreme Court Building, 1-Salamanca Place, Hobart (03)6233-7915

Launceston Law Library, Ground floor, Staffordshire House, 56-Charles Street, Launceston ph. (03)6331-2666

North West Law Library, 1st floor, Supreme Court Building, Alexander Street, Burnie ph. (03)6434-6339

Victoria

Public Law Library (through Victorian Legal Aid), 350-Queen Street, Melbourne ph. 1800-677-402

Websites

Federal government

<www.australia.gov.au>
<www.gov.au>
<www.ag.gov.au>
<www.comlaw.gov.au>

State governments

<www.act.gov.au>
<www.nsw.gov.au>
<www.lawaccess.nsw.gov.au>
<www.lawlink.nsw.gov.au>
<www.liac.sl.nsw.gov.au>
<www.nt.gov.au>
<www.qld.gov.au>
<www.sa.gov.au>
<www.tas.gov.au>
<www.vic.gov.au>
<www.wa.gov.au>

Community legal centres

<www.naclc.org.au>

Legislation and cases

<www.austlii.edu.au>
<www.nsw.lawlink.nsw.gov.au/caselaw>

Other

<www.weblaw.edu.au>
<www.lawmap.com.au>
<www.lawstuff.org.au>

Other contacts

TIS Translating and Interpreting Service ph. 13-14-50
National Relay Service (for people who are deaf, hearing or speech impaired) ph. 13-25-44

Back Cover Material

Designed for those with little or no legal training, this book provides a step-by-step guide to running a non-criminal case in a court or tribunal. Whether you are bringing an action or defending one, it offers practical advice on:

- making a claim
- defending a claim
- collecting evidence
- researching the law
- negotiating a settlement
- presenting a case at a hearing
- whether to appeal the result.

Accompanied by case studies, checklist, tips and an explanation of legal terms, this book applies Australia wide and to all types of civil litigation, including family law, neighbour disputes, debt claims, compensation, tenancy disputes and appealing a government decision.

Index

A
adjournment, *75, 224, 229, 241*
Administrative Appeals Tribunal, see tribunal,
Administrative Decisions Tribunal, see tribunal,
administrative law, *51, 71*
  see also appeal of a government decision,
adversarial approach, *55, 57, 59, 61, 64, 246*
advocate, *31*
affidavit, *59, 85, 94, 136, 161, 165, 167, 187, 189, 209, 220, 222, 232*
  of service, *165*
amending,
  documents, *207*
  the claim, *98, 100*
  the defence, *120*
appeal, *20, 53, 55, 76, 157, 236, 248, 250, 252, 254, 255*
  of a government decision, *9, 20, 51, 62, 85, 87, 120, 140, 144, 196*
applicant, *51, 62, 73, 120, 172, 187, 189, 191, 193, 194, 196, 207*
  see also plaintiff,
application, *16, 31, 41, 51, 73, 75, 81, 83, 85, 87, 89, 91, 92, 94, 96, 98, 100, 102, 107, 187, 189, 191, 214, 250, 252, 254*
  see also claim,
  for review,
  see also appeal of a government decision,
  for leave to appeal, *254*
  to have judgment set aside, *102*

assessing your case, *22, 24, 31, 33, 89, 115, 126, 159*
- its complexity, *20, 22, 24, 25*
- do you have a case at all?, *33*
- should it go to court?, *36, 37, 38, 39*
- should you get a lawyer?, *20, 22, 24, 25, 28, 29, 31*

associate, *236*
AUSTLII, *45, 153, 254*

B

balance of probabilities, *51, 75, 128, 170, 194*
bar, the, *5, 236*
barrister, *5, 11*
Bar table, *57, 59, 236*
bench, the, *57, 236*
beyond reasonable doubt, *49, 51, 75, 128*
binding decision, *53, 153, 155, 255*

builder's warranty case outline, *182, 184, 185*
burden of proof, test of proof, *51, 75, 128*

C

call-over, see hearing,
case citation, *155*
case management conference, *73*
- see also conference,
case outlines, see outline of a case,
case studies,
- conferences, *122, 124*
- Helen's letter, *38*
- Jack trains his lawyer, *13, 14*
- Jed's debt claim, *91, 92*
- Kim's curtains, *109, 111, 113, 115*
- Maria's appeals, *9*

McLibel case, *24, 25*
Murray's boarder, *83*
Robbie gets real, *94*
Thanh gets creative, *107*
Centrelink, *9, 62, 140, 196, 198, 200, 202, 204, 205*
certificate of readiness, *163*
certified copy of a document, *161*
certiorari, *71*
checklist,
  of documents for the hearing, *232*
  for preparing the claim, *94*
  for preparing the defence, *118*
chronology, *87, 91, 94, 102, 104, 111, 118, 172, 174, 229, 232*
civil,
  action, *49*
  see also claim,
  see also application,

burden of proof, *75*
law, litigation, *43, 49, 51, 66, 68*
claim, *31, 33, 38, 49, 51, 59, 66, 70, 73, 75, 81, 83, 85, 87, 89, 91, 92, 94, 96, 98, 100, 102, 104, 106, 107, 109, 115, 117, 118, 124, 128, 132, 152, 157, 159, 161, 163, 167, 170, 172, 174, 175, 177, 179, 180, 182, 184, 185, 216, 218, 225, 227, 232*
  see also application,
claimant, *73*
  see also plaintiff,
claim for liquidated damages,
  see claim,
common law, *53*
community justice centres, *36*
community legal centres, *9, 41, 43*
compliance certificate, *163*
conference, *73, 75, 81, 120, 122, 124, 126*
consumer claim, *66*

case study Jed's debt, *91, 92*
case study Kim's curtains, *109, 111, 113, 115*
preliminary outline, *182, 184, 185*
consumer tribunal, see tribunal,
costs, see legal costs,
costs agreement, *11, 14*
court, *5, 7, 24, 25, 28, 29, 31, 33, 36, 37, 38, 39, 41, 45, 49, 51, 53, 55, 57, 64, 68, 70, 71, 73, 75, 81, 83, 85, 96, 98, 100, 102, 104, 106, 107, 115, 117, 120, 124, 132, 134, 138, 144, 146, 148, 152, 153, 155, 157, 161, 163, 165, 167, 168, 185, 189, 191, 193, 207, 209, 214, 220, 222, 225, 229, 232, 234, 236, 238, 246, 248, 250, 252, 254*
  and self-representation, *25, 28*
  choice between tribunal and, *83*
  Petty Sessions, *55*
  District, *57*
  Family, *28, 55, 96, 98, 107, 153, 157, 185, 191, 193*
  Federal, *55*
  High, *28, 53, 55*
  inferior, *25, 64, 71*
  Local, *25, 51*
  Magistrates, *25, 29, 51, 53, 55*
  Planning and Environment, *28*
  Small Claims, *25, 29, 38, 83*
  superior, *28*
  Supreme, *28, 51, 53, 55, 100, 157, 163*
courtroom, *57, 59, 61, 64, 234, 236, 238*
criminal law, *49, 51, 66*
  burden of proof in, *75*
counter claim, *106, 107, 109*
cross-claim, *106, 107, 109, 118*
cross-examination, *124, 134, 138, 209, 220, 222, 224*

D

damages, *68, 70*
debt claim, *49, 91, 92*
declaration, *70*
default judgment, *73, 100*
defence, *16, 73, 81, 100, 102, 104, 106, 107, 109, 111, 113, 115, 117, 118, 120, 132, 159, 161, 172, 174, 225, 232*
  amended, *120*
defendant in criminal proceedings, *49*
  in non-criminal proceedings, *51, 73*
  see also respondent
decision,
  see also result,
  reserved, *76, 244, 246*
digital images, *132, 134*
directions hearing,
  see hearing,
disbursements, *11*
discovery of documents, *146, 148*
dispute resolution services, *36*
District Court,
  see court,

E

enforcement, *248, 250*
enter an appearance, *100*
equity, *68, 70, 71*
evidence, *87, 89, 91, 94, 104, 106, 109, 113, 124, 126, 128, 130, 132, 134, 136, 138, 140, 142, 144, 146, 148, 150, 152, 174, 175, 182, 184, 187, 189, 196, 198, 200, 207, 209, 211, 213, 216, 220, 222, 224, 225, 227, 232*
  see also facts,
examination-in-chief, *209, 222, 224*
extension of time, *165*

F

fact, *77, 78, 87, 91, 94, 106, 109, 113, 128, 130, 172, 174, 175, 182, 184, 187, 189, 196, 198, 200, 213, 220*
  see also evidence,

how the law applies to the, *78, 128, 150, 211*
issues of, *22, 24, 130*
Family Court,
  see court,
family law, *13, 51, 96, 98, 100, 157, 185, 187, 189, 191, 193, 194, 252*
Federal Court,
  see court federal
government,
  see government,
filing documents, *98, 165, 167, 229*
filing fee, *73, 87, 94, 107, 118, 120, 175, 254*
FOI, Freedom Of Information, *140, 142, 144*
full bench, *55*
further and better particulars, *104, 118*

G

garnishee order,
  see order,
golden rules of litigation, *77, 78, 85, 100, 102, 126, 130, 152, 167, 168, 240, 241, 242, 250*
government, *53, 55*
  documents, *140, 142, 144*

H

hearing, *3, 13, 25, 28, 45, 55, 57, 59, 61, 62, 64, 73, 75, 94, 98, 122, 126, 128, 130, 132, 134, 136, 138, 167, 170, 172, 207, 209, 211, 213, 225, 229, 231, 232, 234, 236, 238, 240, 241, 242*
  call-over, *75*
  date of, *75, 124, 126, 170, 232*
  directions, *75*
  final preparations for the, *229, 231, 232*
  information form, *163*
  mentions, *75*
hearing room, *234, 236, 238*
  see also court room,
hearsay evidence, *148*
High Court,

see court,

I
inferior court,
  see court,
injunction, *70*
inquisitorial approach, *55, 57, 61, 62, 64, 211*
instalments, pay by, *231, 250*
interest, *70, 87, 91, 92, 94, 182*
interim orders,
  see orders
interlocutory orders,
  see orders,
internet, *47, 213*
interrogatories, *146, 148*

J
jurisdiction, *83, 94*
jury, *55*

K
key issues of a case, *20, 22, 172*

L
law,
  how governments make, *53, 55*
  issues of, *22, 24*
  types of, *49, 51*
  see also legal,
Law Society, *7, 16, 18, 41*
law textbooks, *47, 153*
lawyer, *2, 5, 7, 9, 11, 13, 14, 16, 18, 20, 22, 24, 25, 28, 29, 31*
  changing your, *13, 14, 16*
  complaints about, *16, 18*
  first appointment with your, *11, 13*
  instructing your, *13, 14*
  other party's, *18, 231, 240, 254*
  pro bono, *43, 255*
  tips for choosing, *9, 11, 13*
lawyer–client relationship, *14*

leading questions, *220, 222, 224*
leave to appeal, *252*
   to apply out of time, *165*
legal,
  advice, *18, 31, 33, 41, 43, 45, 47, 68, 71, 83, 87, 89, 98, 104, 106, 111, 126, 148, 152, 153, 155, 159, 168, 246, 254*
  argument, *57, 59, 89, 92, 94, 109, 113, 117, 118, 174, 179, 180, 184, 185, 191, 193, 194, 202, 204, 207, 209, 211, 214, 240, 254, 255*
  see also submissions,
  costs, *29, 37, 89, 117, 148, 161, 231, 232, 252, 254*
  see also no costs jurisdiction,
  information compared to advice, *41, 43, 45*
  documents, *161, 163, 165, 167, 168*
  jargon, *7, 128, 167, 168*
  remedies, *64, 66, 68, 70, 71, 87, 96, 174*
  requirements of a case, *87, 89, 91, 94, 104, 109, 111, 118, 150, 152, 214*
  research, *45, 47, 87, 96, 104, 106, 111, 118, 128, 150, 152, 153, 155, 157, 159, 161*
  system, *25, 33, 36, 37, 49, 51, 53, 55, 57, 59, 61, 62, 64, 66, 68, 70, 71*
Legal Aid, *7, 41, 43, 255*
letter of demand, *38, 39, 91*
limitation period or date, *83, 94*
  see also time limits,
litigation process, the, *73, 75, 76*
Local Court,
  see court local government,
  see government lower court,
  see court, inferior,

M

Magistrates Court,
  see court main outline,
  see outline of a case,
mandamus, *71*
mediation, *73, 122*
  see also conference,
medical records, *140, 144*
mentions hearing,
  see hearing,
merits of a case, *3, 16, 31, 33, 126, 159*
mitigation, minimisation of loss, *70, 180*
motion,
  see notice of motion,

N

non-criminal law,
  see civil law no,
costs jurisdiction, *24, 37*
notice of,
  appeal, *254*
  discontinuance, *163*
  motion, *31, 163*
  withdrawal, *163*
non-government information, *144*

O

ombudsman, *36*
online lodgement, *85, 117, 213*
order(s), *75, 87, 92, 98, 106, 144, 175, 182, 185, 187, 189, 193, 194, 231, 244, 246, 248, 250*
  garnishee, *250*
  interim, *75*
  interlocutory, *75*
  preliminary, *75*
  set aside, *87, 102, 196, 248*
outline of a case, *170, 172, 174, 175, 177, 179, 180, 182, 184, 185, 187, 189, 191, 193, 194, 196, 198, 200, 202, 204, 205, 213, 214, 216, 218, 225, 227, 229, 232*

main, *170, 213, 214, 216, 218, 229, 232*
preliminary, *170, 172, 174, 175, 177, 179, 180, 182, 184, 185, 187, 189, 191, 193, 194, 196, 198, 200, 202, 204, 205, 232*
summarised, *225, 227, 232*
outline of a case, examples,
  applicant's case in an appeal of a government decision, *196, 198, 200, 202, 204, 205*
  plaintiff's case in a consumer matter, *182, 184, 185, 216, 218*
  plaintiff's case in a tenancy dispute, *175, 177, 179, 180, 182*
  respondent's case in a family law matter, *185, 187, 189, 191, 193, 194*

P

photographs, *92, 104, 132, 134, 177, 180, 184, 216, 227*
plaintiff, *51, 59, 73, 75, 100, 124, 128, 130, 163, 170, 172, 175, 182, 207, 209, 213*
police reports, *140, 144*
precedent, *53*
preliminary conference,
  see conference,
preliminary orders,
  see order(s), *75*
preliminary outlines,
  see outline of a case,
prerogative writs, *71*
privacy legislation, *144*
  see outline of a case,
  see lawyer,
prohibition, *71*

R

re-examination, *209, 222*
registrar, *45*

remedies,
   see legal remedies,
reserved decision, *76, 211, 244, 246*
respondent, *51, 59, 73, 124, 128, 130, 170, 172, 174, 179, 182, 184, 207, 209, 213*
response,
   see defence
   result, *73, 244, 246, 248, 250*
   see also decision,
rules of evidence, *148, 150, 224*

S

self-representation, *2, 3, 29, 64*
serving documents, *94, 98, 100, 118, 120, 165, 229*
settling a case, *33, 73, 75, 115, 117, 126, 159, 229*
small claims matter, *38, 83*
Small Claims Court,
   see court,
Social Security Appeals Tribunal,
   see tribunal,
solicitor, *5*
   see also lawyer,
specific performance, *70*
state government,
   see government
statement contesting the application,
   see defence,
statement of claim, *59, 85*
   see also application,
   see also claim,
statement of facts and contentions, *163*
statement of issues, *163*
statutory declaration, *161*
stay of proceedings, *252*
strike-out application or motion, *31*
subpoena, *134, 146, 148*

submissions, *209, 211, 213, 214, 218, 227, 232*
success in litigation, *77, 78, 130, 246, 248*
summarised outline,
  see outline of a case,
summons, *134*
superior court,
  see court,
Supreme Court,
  see court,

T

T docs, *120, 198*
tenancy, *20, 49, 68, 175, 177, 179, 180, 182, 227*
Tenancy Tribunal,
  see tribunal,
tendering documents, *167, 207, 209, 211, 222, 225, 227, 229*
test of proof,
  see burden of proof,
time limits, *45, 76, 78, 83, 100, 102, 104, 165, 167, 229, 248, 252, 254*

tribunal, *25, 28, 29, 45, 51, 53, 55, 62, 64, 66, 71, 73, 75, 81, 83, 85, 91, 94, 98, 100, 102, 104, 106, 107, 111, 117, 120, 122, 124, 132, 134, 136, 146, 153, 155, 157, 161, 163, 165, 177, 207, 209, 211, 220, 225, 227, 229, 236, 238, 248, 252*
  Administrative Appeals, *9, 55, 64, 66, 252*
  Administrative Decisions, *64*
  and self-representation, *25, 28*
  and the rules of evidence, *148, 150, 220*
  appeals, *28*
  choice between court and, *83*
  consumer, *66, 91, 92, 111*
  inquisitorial approach of, *62, 64*
  review, *28*
  Social Security Appeals, *9, 62, 64*

Tenancy, *49, 153*

U
university libraries, *47*

V
video, *132, 134*
  link-up, *134, 138*

W
waiver of fees, *87, 94, 109, 118, 120, 142, 254*
without prejudice, *115, 117*
witness(es), *75, 106, 124, 134, 136, 138, 140, 207, 209, 220, 222, 224, 225, 229, 232, 236, 241*
  expenses, *134, 138*
  expert, *136, 138, 140*
  statement, *136, 161, 220, 222, 232*
written costs agreement,
  see costs agreement,

Y
Your Honour, *236*

Your Worship, *236*

www.ingramcontent.com/pod-product-compliance
Ingram Content Group UK Ltd.
Pitfield, Milton Keynes, MK11 3LW, UK
UKHW041208180426
11947UKWH00023B/1936